How to use this book to your best advantage.

In the first section of the book, look for the answers to these provocative questions ...

• What are the different applications of Sulky products for applique and when, where, why and how do I use each one?

• How do I use Color Theory and the Sulky Thread Palette in applique?

In the largest section, look for exciting, stimulating, creative **Projects & Tips** from top name creative Instructors, Authors and TV Sewing Stars in our industry.

You will find appliqued projects for men, women, children and babies that feature individual and combined uses of Sulky Threads, Sulky Stabilizers, Sulky Puffy Foam, Sulky Iron-on Heat Transfer Pens and Sulky KK 2000 Temporary Spray Adhesive.

In the last section, you will find **Quick Projects and Sources** for hard-to-find patterns, notions, etc., used in the projects.

Plus a Big Bonus!
4 huge 42" x 45" Pattern Sheets with full-size designs and 2 bonus projects!

Introduction to Sulky Secrets to Successful Decorating using Sulky Decorative Threads and Stabilizers!

by Joyce Drexler

• What Sulky Threads can we use for Applique?

To those who have never used Sulky Threads either by hand, for machine-fed or free-motion applique, they are a beautiful discovery that makes applique even more enjoyable and creative. Virtually all Sulky Threads make the vibrant end result of any of our creative applique projects exactly what we envisioned when we conceived them.

• When should we use Sulky Threads & Stabilizers for Appliqueing?

The broad range of Sulky Threads and stabilizers help you add your extra special touch to virtually any type of applique . . . Hand, Machine-Fed and Free-Motion.

• Where should we use Sulky Threads for Applique?

For "invisible applique", Sulky Polyester Invisible Thread is the thread most professionals prefer to use to achieve the best, long-lasting results because it is made of 100% polyester instead of nylon, giving it a more flexible, soft touch, and making it more tolerant to the heat of an iron.

The rest of the Sulky Decorative thread line should be used wherever and whenever you want your applique stitching to be beautifully visible with unique color interest. Hand and Machine Appliquers love the extraordinarily smooth finish on Sulky Rayon, Cotton, Polyester and Metallic Threads which allows them to glide easily through fabric. Use Sulky 35 wt. UltraTwist™ Rayon anywhere that you want to create unbelievable tone, texture and dimension.

The brilliance of Sulky **"Sliver" Metallic and the <u>NEW</u> Sulky Hologram-effect Metallic called "Holoshimmer"** is wonderful for adding eye-catching pizazz to any applique project.

For those of us who love the country fabric lines of Moda, M & M Fabrics by Debbie Mumm and RJR's Thimbleberries, Sulky has 30 wt. & 40 wt. Rayon Multi-color threads (#2207, #2208 & #2210) that match perfectly! There are also Sulky Multi-color threads (#2204 & #2205) for jewel tones like the Cherrywood Hand-Dyed Fabrics.

Of course, Sulky's <u>NEW</u> Cotton Thread in both 30 wt. and very thick 12 wt. is ideal for creating a more matte, country look to appliqued quilts, wallhangings and garments.

Available in 66 colors in both weights, Sulky Cotton has the perfect palette for hand-work, primitive outline work, red-work, machine blanket-stitch and satin-stitch applique, quilting, specialty embroidery, and free-motion stitching. A truly new and exciting addition to the already extraordinary line of Sulky threads.

Meet the Author and read on to learn the Sulky Applique Secrets . . .

Joyce Drexler

Instructor, Artist, Quilter, Author, Designer, and Executive Vice President of Sulky of America, Inc., as well as Co-Owner of the mail order company, Speed Stitch, Inc. from Port Charlotte, FL

Joyce is widely recognized as a leader in the field of "Machine Arts and Crafts". Since 1979 she has taught several thousand Retailers and Teachers in Instructor Training Workshops across America and Canada.

Her books have sold well over 500,000 copies and are also being sold internationally. She is the producer and co-author of the popular Sulky Book Series *"Concepts in Sulky"*, plus *"Sulky Secrets to Successful Stabilizing"* and *"Sulky Secrets to Successful Quilting"*.

Joyce has been published in numerous magazines, and she appears regularly on the PBS TV Programs: *Sew Creative; America Sews with Sue Hausmann; Creative Living; Sew Perfect; Quilting From the Heartland; Kaye's Quilting Friends; Fons & Porter; Quilt Central; and Martha's Sewing Room.*

She also designed a one-of-a-kind garment for the prestigious Fairfield Fashion Show.

She creates the projects for the Sulky of America *"Sew Exciting Seminars"* and collaborates with Patsy Shields to teach the Sulky Educators that travel nationally conducting these Seminars. She also coordinates the Annual Sulky Challenge that offers prizes valued at over $64,000.

Joyce also has illustrated her own designs to create embroidery cards in the Designer Series for both Amazing Designs®: "Inspirational Concepts in Sulky" - AD3000; "Four Seasons - Ultra Twist" - AD3002; Seasonal "Embroideryscapes" - ES202; "Inspirational Concepts in Sulky - Pressed Leaves" - AD3009; and for Cactus Punch®: "Autumn" Designer Series 77, ("Spring" Designer Series 78, "Summer" Designer Series 79, and "Winter" Designer Series 80 - coming soon).

In 1999, Joyce received the prestigious "Schmetz Golden Needle Award" in acknowledgement of her significant contributions toward enhancing the future of the sewing industry.

• Why do we want to use Sulky Threads for Appliqueing?

There are over 385 colors of soft, warm, natural-looking Sulky Rayon Threads available, so it is easy to choose just the right solid color, variegated shade, multi-color or Ultra Twist thread for any applique project.

However, cotton was and is the applique and quilting thread of choice for many years, and Sulky now has the new matte-finish *Sulky Cotton* in both 30 wt. and the much heavier 12 wt. Both are available in 66 luscious colors.

On the other hand, appliqued projects that are used daily will also last longer when stitched with Sulky Rayon and Polyester threads rather than cotton and nylon. Sulky Poly Deco™ is a Polyester Decorative Thread that is colorfast even when using detergents with optical brighteners or bleach. So, if you are making an appliqued baby quilt, toddler quilt or clothing, or something appliqued for teenagers and college-age kids, using Sulky Poly Deco will still give you the shine close to Rayon plus the added durability of Polyester.

• How do we use Sulky Threads for Appliqueing?

This is what you will learn in this book from the numerous, diversified, creative projects and tips. We will be discussing practical applications and guidelines for decorative thread usage for applique.

Use this book as a source of inspiration, reference and information. If you have more ideas that we haven't touched on, we would love to hear from you. Maybe your tip or idea can be included in our next book.

Write, Fax or E-Mail Sulky:

SULKY OF AMERICA, INC.
3113 Broadpoint Dr, Dept. B-14
Punta Gorda, FL 33983
FAX: 941-743-4634

CONSUMER RELATIONS
E-mail: info@sulky.com
Visit our **website:**
www.sulky.com

A Beginner's Quick Reference Guide to using SULKY® Threads for Applique by Machine or Free-Motion

Type of Sulky Thread	Solid Colors available	Variegated Colors available	Multi-Colors available	Type and Size Needle to use	Spool Pin vertical	Spool Pin horizontal	Top Tension	Can be used in Bobbin	Yardage on Regular Spool	Yardage on King Size Spool
30 wt. Rayon	102	36	18	Quilting or Top Stitch 90 or 100	ok	ok	Loosen Slightly	yes	180	500
40 wt. Rayon	283	36	18	Embroidery 75 or 90	ok	ok	Loosen Slightly	yes	250	850
35 wt. UltraTwist™	50	0	0	Quilting or Topstitch 14/90	ok	ok	Loosen Slightly	yes	200	700
40 wt. Poly Deco™	138	0	0	Embroidery 75 or 90	ok	ok	Loosen Slightly	ok	250	900
Original Metallic	27	0	9	Metallic or Topstitch 14/90	ok	ok	Loosen a lot	yes with care	165 except multi-colors	1000
Sliver™ Metallic	22	0	2	Metallic or Topstitch 14/90	must	no	Very Loose	yes with care	250	N/A
Holoshimmer Metallic *New!*	22	0	2	Metallic or Topstitch 14/90	must	no	Very Loose	yes with care	250	N/A
12 wt. Cotton *New!*	66	0	0	Quilting or Topstitch 90 or 100	ok	ok	Loosen Slightly	yes	N/A	330
30 wt. Cotton *New!*	66	0	0	Quilting or Topstitch 14/90	ok	ok	Loosen Slightly	yes	N/A	500
Polyester Invisible	2	0	0	Quilting 75 or 90	ok	ok	Loosen Slightly	yes wind slowly	440	2400
Polyester Bobbin	2	0	0	N/A	ok	ok	N/A	yes	475	1500

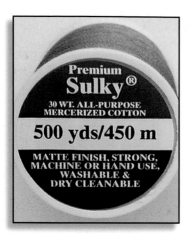

New! *Sulky* 30 wt. Cotton Decorative Applique Threads!

Now you can have Sulky quality and a matte finish of cotton thread for that homespun look. Premier Quality, long staple, highly mercerized Egyptian Cotton with a matte finish to create a soft, warm, natural look and feel.

Perfect for:
- *Machine or Hand Applique*
- *Hand or Machine Quilting and Piecing*
- *Computerized Redwork*
- *Machine Embroidery & Monogramming*
- *Couching • Tassels • Fringe*
- *Lace Work • Bobbin Work*
- *Machine Decorative Stitches*
- *All Purpose Sewing*
- *Long-Arm Quilting*
- *Serger Techniques*
- *Counted Cross Stitch*
- *French Hand Work*

Because all Sulky Cotton Thread is made from the highest quality, highly mercerized Egyptian Cotton available in the world, you will not have problems with thread breaking, unraveling or deteriorating as a result of poor quality thread. Over 50 years of engineering and research has gone into perfecting the performance of today's Sulky Cotton Decorative Thread. From raw goods to twisting, and from dyeing to finishing, all ingredients of thread manufacturing are combined perfectly to produce the smoothest Sulky Cotton Thread that is still strong enough to survive today's machine evolution.

Look for the brown label which is exclusively on Sulky 30 wt. Cotton Thread.
See Sources page 164 if you can not find this new thread locally.

New! 66 beautiful colors of 30 wt. Cotton Thread on 500 yd. KING Snap-end Spools.

- *Ideal for use on a sewing machine, embroidery machine, serger, long-arm quilting machine, or for hand use.*
- *No more thread falling off the spool and tangling under the spool pin.*
- *No more unprotected, exposed thread at the end of the spool or cone that can become trapped by the spool holder.*
- *No more tangled messes in your thread storage box.*
- *No more spools or cones that don't turn smoothly and evenly on vertical spool pins.*

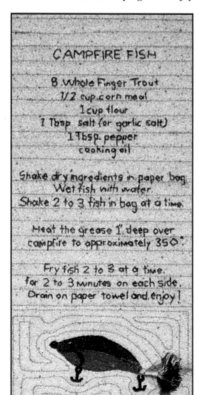

Built-in Decorative Blanket Stitch Applique by Machine and beautiful Hand Embroidery Work by Patti Lee. See pages 68-69 for instructions to make this ideal gift for the Fisherman in your life.

Sulky 12 wt. "The Extra Thick One" New! Cotton Decorative Thread!

Sulky 12 wt. Cotton is a natural fiber that has very much the same thickness as some pearl cottons, but can flow through a size 14/90 or 16/100 machine needle, therefore it is ideal for Applique by Hand or Machine.

Available in 66 Matte Colors on 330 yd. Sulky King Snap-end Spools for the easiest thread flow. Wind it on the bobbin for Machine Bobbin Work. Thread your hand needle with as many strands as desired for the look of floss, but with the ease and convenience of a spool. Use for Counted Cross Stitch, Hand Embroidery and Crewel Work.

Premier Quality, long staple, highly mercerized Egyptian Cotton with a matte finish to create a soft, warm, natural look and feel.

66 Perfect Colors that are ideal for Primitives, Antique and Country looks.

This wallhanging, inspired by Jenny Haskins, was created by Jan Brostek, owner of Pins & Needles in Middleburg Hts., OH. She used Sulky 12 wt. Cotton, free-motion, applique, and decorative stitches on a Pfaff 7570. Some designs were done directly on the wallhanging and others were appliqued on later.

- Because of Sulky 12 wt. Cotton's matte finish and quality, it will glide smoothly through a quilt top, batting and backing when stitched either by hand or machine.

- Appliqueing with Sulky Cotton Thread will give you the soft, warm, natural looking results that you desire.

- Sulky color numbers are printed on each spool's **orange** label.

- Other Beautiful Uses:
  - Hand or Machine Redwork
  - Low Density Computerized Embroidery
  - Machine Decorative Stitches
  - Serger Techniques • Top Stitching
  - Couching • Tassels • Fringe

- Sulky Cotton is completely Machine Washable in either hot or cold water. Use a laundry soap or detergent that does <u>not</u> contain chlorine or optical brighteners.

- Sulky Cotton is Dry Cleanable.

180 yds.

500 yds.

Sulky 30 wt. "Heavy" Rayon Decorative Applique Threads!

1/3 Thicker than 40 wt., 2/3 Thicker than 50 wt. for greater visibility, depth and unique color interest in Applique Stitches.

Available in 156 Luscious Colors - 102 solid and 54 Variegated and Multi-Colors on both a 180 yd. and 500 yd. snap spool.

King Snap-end Spools:
- *No more thread falling off the spool and tangling under the spool pin.*

- *No more unprotected, exposed thread at the end of the spool or cone that can become trapped by the spool holder.*

- *No more need to use thread nets.*

- *No more tangled messes in your thread storage boxes with Sulky's snap-spools.*

- *No more spools or cones that don't turn smoothly and evenly on vertical spool pins.*

Because all Sulky Rayon Thread is made from the highest quality technical raw goods available in the world, you will not have problems with thread breaking, unraveling or deteriorating as a result of poor quality thread. Over 50 years of engineering and research has gone into perfecting the performance of today's Sulky Rayon Threads.

From raw goods to twisting, and from dyeing to finishing, all ingredients of thread manufacturing are combined perfectly to produce the shiny, smooth Sulky Thread that is still strong enough to survive today's machine evolution. Look for the red label or red printing on the spool which is exclusively for Sulky 30 wt. Rayon Thread.

Part of the Bear Clan Totem Pole Vest by Sharon Boysen from the Book Art. 900B-13, "Sulky Secrets to Successful Quilting". Sulky 30 wt. Rayon was used to blanket stitch applique.

6

Sulky 40 wt. "Light but Strong" Decorative Applique Threads!

Sulky 40 wt. Rayon is a man-made fiber that has very much the same luster as silk, and silk's smoothness, but is stronger than both silk and cotton thread, and therefore is perfect for applique by hand or machine.

Satin Stitch appliqueing with Sulky 40 wt. Rayon produces a beautiful satiny bead of stitching in which individual stitches are barely visible.

Available in 337 Vibrant Colors - 283 Solid Colors and 54 Variegated and Multi-Colors on both a 250 yd. and 850 yd. Snap-end Spool.

If you love to do machine embroidery, you should know that the vast majority of embroidery designs are digitized for 40 wt. Rayon. Because of its excellent runability, unparalleled quality, and huge selection of colors, Sulky is the first choice of home embroiderers. Sulky 40 wt. Rayon is also easier to use than polyester because it has less stretch and stretch memory. Sulky Rayon lays down nicely in the design without the occasional thread pull-ups which occur when using polyester. Sulky 40 wt. Rayon's look is more soft, warm and natural compared to the almost "plasticky" look of polyester. Because of polyester's added, unnecessary strength, it causes the acceleration of wear on the machine's moving parts and thread path.

- Because of Sulky's silky finish and legendary quality, it will smoothly glide through a quilt top, batting and backing when stitched either by hand or machine.

- Sulky Rayon does <u>not</u> fray and fuzz in the machine, and it does <u>not</u> shrink like cotton.

- Sulky Rayon is cross-wound on the small spool to ensure easier thread flow on any machine, and consistently superior stitch quality.

- Sulky has color numbers and weight sizes printed in black ink on each small spool for easy identification.

- Sulky Rayon is completely Machine Washable in either hot or cold water. Use a laundry soap or detergent that does <u>not</u> contain chlorine or optical brighteners.

- Sulky Rayon is Dry Cleanable.

Computer Embroidered Applique by Machine using one of the new designs from "Seasonal Embroideryscapes" designed by Joyce Drexler for Amazing Designs (ES202).
See Sources on page 164.

Sulky Premium Polyester Invisible Applique Threads!

- Perfect for invisible applique, machine "hand-look" quilting, and stitching in the ditch. *Ideal for hems too!*
- Very fine .004 monofilament that is soft enough for baby quilts or garments that will be worn next to the skin.
- Wonderful to use as a lightweight bobbin thread for decorative stitches and embroidery. Compatible with Sulky Metallics, Rayons, Cottons and Poly Deco.
- Available in both smoke for darker fabrics and clear for lighter fabrics.
- Has no rough edges on the spool to tangle, snarl, or break the thread.
  Because it is 100% polyester, it does not melt with normal ironing through the cotton setting.

Sulky Invisible Monofilament Thread is made of 100% Polyester instead of nylon, making it softer, more flexible, and more tolerant to the heat of any iron.

Available in a 440 yd. or 2,400 yd. snap-end spool which makes it easy to find the end, and neat and tidy to store. Spool turns easily on vertical and horizontal spool pins without thread spilling off.

Sulky Premium Invisible was used for these turned-edge Pansy Appliques by Trish Liden, National Sulky Educator from California.

8

Sulky 40 wt. Poly Deco ™ Polyester Applique Thread

Sulky 40 wt. Poly Deco is a top quality, strong, 100% polyester, shiny thread that is especially suited for applique and embroidery on children's clothing, work clothes, sport clothes, or any garment that will need to be washed frequently.

Unlike rayon, Poly Deco can be laundered with soap containing optical brighteners and bleach. Since Poly Deco has more stretch and stretch memory than Rayon, the top tension generally has to be reduced, and the type and amount of stabilizer(s) can be different than when using Rayon. Strong enough to be used to sew seams together.

Sulky Poly Deco was used in this "Solvy-turned", appliqued Chicken Quilt, by Evelyn Howard. Evelyn also loves to use Sulky Poly Deco for hand stitching the bindings of quilts, because of the silky texture of the thread. She says, "It flows like butter with no tangling or trouble." (See pages 60-63 for instructions.) Quilted with Sulky 30 wt. Rayons.

9

Sulky Original Metallic Thread!

Sulky Original Metallic Thread is a round, twisted thread that is available in 36 solid and multi-colors that are made by wrapping the finest metallic foil around a strong core to produce a soft, smooth thread that easily glides through your applique projects.

*Metallic Thread is ideal even for Sheer Applique like the table scarf below created by Viking Education Consultant, Alix Graham-Michel, using a 14/90 needle and Sulky Metallic #7007 Gold on both the top and in the bobbin. Since organza is a very stable fabric, she used Sulky Solvy as the stabilizer for the embroidery and Tear-Easy for the embroidery on the Silk Dupioni. The design is from the Martha Pullen Card, "Flowers and Frames 2" and the monogram is from the Kalligraphia Font which comes with the Designer I and II. Metallic Thread adds that special sparkle to all appliques including Sulky #7028 Multi-colored Metallic used on the satin Angel Wings of the beautiful applique below by Ellen Osten. The creative Bird print applique was satin stitched on a vest by Mary Lou Stark using Sulky #7024 Multi-colored Metallic. Both projects are from the Book Art. 900B-8, **Embellishing Concepts in Sulky.***

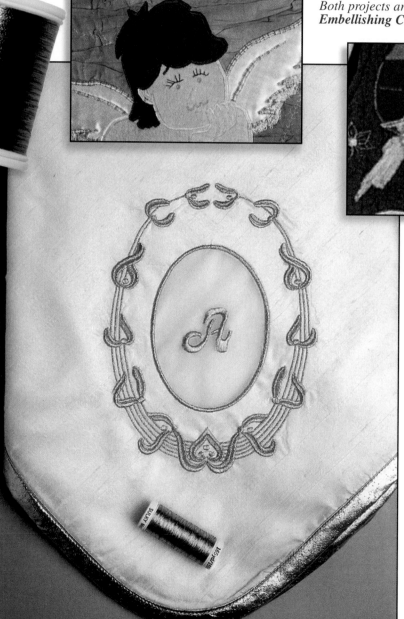

Hints for success with Metallic Threads:

- Use a 14/90 metallic, topstitch, or embroidery needle. Needles that are labeled "for metallic threads" still should be 14/90's.
- Reduce top tension.
- Sew slower.
- Stabilize properly with a soft, non-abrasive Sulky Stabilizer.
- Use a lightweight Sulky Thread in the bobbin, either a matching Sulky 40 wt. Rayon, Sulky Bobbin Thread or Polyester Invisible Thread.
- Dry clean or wash in cool or warm water. Avoid chlorine bleach or other optical brighteners. Iron on low temperature with the right side down on a padded surface; cover with a press cloth.

Sulky SLIVER™ Metallic Applique Thread!

**Available in 24 brilliant solid and multi-colors.
Sliver is a thin, flat, ribbon-like polyester film
that is metalized with aluminum
to make it brilliantly reflective.**

Hints for success when using Sliver:

- Use a 14/90 metallic, topstitch, or embroidery needle. Needles that are labeled "for metallic threads" still should be 14/90's.
- It is important to use Sliver on a **vertical** spool pin since Sliver is a flat thread; the twisting action from unwinding off a horizontal spool pin can cause breakage.
- Sew slower.
- All Metallics hate abrasion and small stitches because Metallics simply don't bend well into small stitches.
- Use a soft, pliable Sulky Stabilizer to properly stabilize your fabric.
- Lower your top tension substantially. On some machines this may mean near "0".
- Use a lightweight Sulky thread in the bobbin, either a matching Sulky 40 wt. Rayon, Sulky Bobbin Thread or Sulky Polyester Invisible Thread.
- Dry clean or Machine wash in cool or warm water, dry at low heat settings. Iron on a low temperature with the right side down on a padded surface; cover with a press cloth.

In the photo to the right, Sulky Sliver Metallic really sets off this Trapunto, free-motion embellished, appliqued, fabric print, Zebra vest, by Carol Ingram.

See step-by-step instructions in the Sulky book, **"Dimensional Concepts in Sulky"**, Art. 900B-12. (See Sources page 164.)

11

New! Sulky Holoshimmer™ Metallic Applique Thread!

Available in 24 brilliant solid and multi-colors. Sulky Holoshimmer is a thin, flat, ribbon-like polyester film that is metalized with an aluminum holographic layer to give it a shimmery, brilliant reflectiveness.

Hints for success when using Holoshimmer:

- Use a 14/90 metallic, topstitch, or embroidery needle. Needles that are labeled "for metallic threads" still need to be 14/90 for Holoshimmer.
- It is important to use Holoshimmer only on a **vertical** spool pin since Holoshimmer is a flat thread; the twisting action from unwinding off a horizontal spool pin can cause breakage.
- Sew slower.
- All Metallics hate abrasion and small stitches because Metallics simply don't bend well into small stitches.
- Use a soft, pliable Sulky Stabilizer to properly stabilize your fabric.
- Lower your top tension substantially. On some machines this may mean near "0".
- Use a lightweight Sulky thread in the bobbin, either a matching Sulky 40 wt. Rayon, Sulky Bobbin Thread or Sulky Polyester Invisible Thread.
- Dry clean or wash in cool or warm water, dry at low heat setting. Iron on a low temperature with the right side down on a padded surface; cover with a press cloth.

24 HOT new Holographic Colors, including two fabulous Multi-colors!

Sulky Holoshimmer Metallic (left) really makes these snowflake, cut-work appliques sparkle with life.

See instructions for this project by Nancy Cornwell on pages 104-108.

Fabric Credit: David Textiles' Polar Fleece designed by Nancy Cornwell. Jacket Pattern - Stretch & Sew #1025.

922-3013
1115/1108

922-3015
1115/1109

922-3023
1109/1219

922-3006
1109/1005

922-3011
1001/1080

922-3021
1080/1219

922-3003
1032/1005

922-3014
1037/1115

922-3020
1037/1219

922-3047
1037/1215

922-3008
1065/1001

922-3031
1065/1067

922-3043
1024/1037

922-3012
1024/1001

922-3049
1025/1023

922-3035
1065/1057

922-3042
1024/1057

922-3000
1065/1005

922-3037
1055/1247

922-3046
1070/1234

922-3028
1204/1045

922-3029
1204/1503

922-3030
1204/1230

922-3001
1045/1005

922-3018
1022/1219

922-3019
1219/1170

922-3022
1166/1219

922-3039
1028/1029

922-3016
1534/1219

922-3048
1044/1535

922-3010
1055/1001

922-3009
1025/1001

922-3038
1237/1056

922-3036
1055/1057

922-3034
1082/1179

922-3007
1082/1005

922-3032
1247/1170

922-3033
1170/1215

922-3004
1005/1170

922-3005
1247/1005

922-3017
1219/1067

922-3041
1063/1049

922-3044
1024/1101

922-3035
1070/1051

922-3025
1055/1208

922-3040
1063/1051

922-3024
1022/1208

922-3027
1208/1049

922-3026
1208/1101

922-3002
1208/1005

Everybody Loves...

Sulky UltraTwist

• 50 Colors • 200 yds. • Silky Sheen • 35 wt. Rayon • Sulky Quality

Add texture to all your embroidery and decorative stitching!

Put a new Twist on your next Appliqued Project!

Because each of the 50 Sulky UltraTwist shades is made by twisting together two existing Sulky solid colored strands, you can stitch UltraTwist individually or use it to accent, highlight, or blend with either or both solid colors to create unbelievable tone, texture and dimension in your applique projects. (The two solid color numbers are printed on the end of the spool.)

Each color family has several shades of UltraTwist so you can create different, dramatic shading effects within the same project. Great for applique, free-motion embroidery and quilting.

Add realism to animals, plants and flowers with the soft shaded look of UltraTwist. Joyce Drexler has designed a seasonal computer embroidery pack that uses UltraTwist exclusively. To the left are just two of over 20 designs offered in the Embroidery Card AD3002 by Amazing Designs™.

Create seasonal appliqued gift bags or covers for jars, baby wipes, etc. Simply embroider the design as usual. Remove the stabilizer. Trim the foundation fabric into a cute shape and blanket stitch it onto a seasonal fabric. Wrap the fabric around the gift, centering the appliqued design in front; tie with a pretty ribbon. The perfect gift idea!

13

Applique Techniques & Supplies

Let's look at the different techniques of applique and how to achieve success with each by using the appropriate Sulky stabilizers and threads. The patterns in the back of this book that require tracing on a fusible web have already been drawn in reverse for your convenience. Add seam allowance to patterns if doing turned applique.

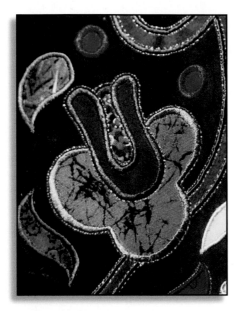

A close-up from a 2001 Sulky Challenge 3rd place winning entry, Jacobean "Wrap"sody by Marjorie Holloway, which employs a unique additional straight stitch outline around the satin stitching.

Changing the Width of your Satin Stitch while Sewing.

In order to change the width of the stitch while sewing, you will need to control the fabric with your left hand. The fore and middle fingers of the left hand should be held in a "V" on either side of the presser foot. With your right hand on the width selector, continuously change the width as the fabric moves forward, making large and small gradations. This technique is often used to produce detail or accent on appliques as in tapering points on leaves.

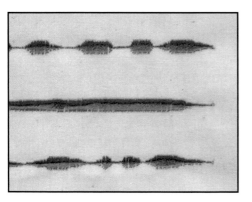

Satin Stitch Method by Machine

Let's study and analyze concave (inner) and convex (outer) curves, points and corners. In practicing these simple stitching techniques, even your first attempt will be charming and pleasing to the eye! But allow yourself time to learn and make a few mistakes along the way --- that is what practice is all about. You will improve with more experience as you do in any new endeavor. Let's plan ahead on how to best handle the shapes. Satin stitch applique is used to cover the raw edges of an applique. Use any of the Sulky Thread types for this technique except Sulky Invisible Polyester Thread. The most commonly used are Sulky 30 wt., 35 wt., and 40 wt. Rayon and Sulky 12 wt. and 30 wt. Cotton.

Pivoting

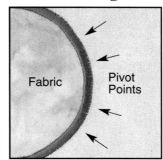

Fabric | Pivot Points

Pivot Points | Fabric

Outside Curves
Pivot when the needle is in the fabric on its right-hand swing. On an outside curve, the needle is on the outside of the appliqued fabric. Remember, the tighter the curve, the more frequently you must pivot. The wider the width of the stitch, the more you will need to pivot. The narrower the width of the stitch, the less pivoting points.

Inside Curves
Pivot when the needle is in the fabric on its left-hand swing. On an inside curve, the needle is on the inside of the appliqued fabric. Remember, in both cases, the edge of the fabric is like a line, and the line should always be vertical to the swing of the needle.

Pivoting on Curves

For most curves, you will not need to stop your machine to pivot; just gently guide around the curved line. But if you do need to stop --- leave the needle in the fabric, lift the presser foot, reposition the fabric, lower the presser foot and continue to stitch. When satin stitching, you have two possible pivot points, on the right-hand swing of the needle or the left-hand swing. Pivoting with the needle on the incorrect side will result in gaps in the stitching line. Pivoting correctly lets the thread stack up slightly, creating a solid line of even, full stitches. By not pivoting at all, the stitching becomes slanted, the width appears uneven, and the resulting look is unattractive and may leave raw edges exposed.

Satin Stitch Appliqueing & Pivoting the Convex or Outer Curve

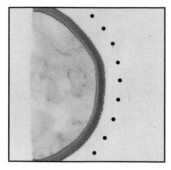

Set the machine to a medium-wide satin stitch. Leave the needle (on its right-hand swing) on the outside of the fabric at the curve, as the dot on the illustration emphasizes. This technique allows the zig-zag stitches to overlap slightly on the inside, shorter curve of the satin stitching. Virtually all of the stitching is on the applique piece. When satin stitching the curve of a design, follow the edge until you notice that the stitches are starting to slant. You will need to turn your applique slightly, or "pivot" every few stitches, while keeping the lines of the curve as vertical as possible. Pivot by stopping with the needle always on the OUTSIDE SWING...on the longer side. You want to cover all the raw edges of the applique and still keep your stitching as wide as when you first began.

Satin Stitch Appliqueing & Pivoting the Concave or Inner Curve

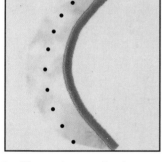

With this technique, you end up with a much tighter curve, but you have to pivot more often. The outside of the curve will be on the applique itself...so the pivoting is done on the applique rather than on the base fabric. Leave the needle in the fabric (on its left-hand swing) at the inside of the curve, as the dot on the illustration emphasizes. Remember, always pivot on the longer side.

Satin Stitch Appliqueing & Pivoting the Outside Square Corner

Knowing just a few tricks makes it easy! Start midway between the corners. Never start your stitching at a corner if possible. Satin Stitch, allowing the right-hand

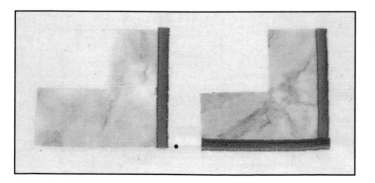

swing of the needle to fall just into the base fabric. Stitch until the needle is just off the point of the corner. With the needle in the fabric on its right-hand swing, pivot the fabric so the second leg is now vertical and in front of the needle. Turn the handwheel toward you to be sure the next swing of the needle will be lined up squarely with your first row of stitching; then satin stitch the next side. *Hint: Because you will be stitching over satin stitching at the corner, you may need to help the fabric move a little as you start to sew the second leg.*

Satin Stitch Appliqueing the Inside Square Corner

This technique is done the same as the outside square corner, except you have to form your own corner. Stitch beyond the corner the actual width of your satin stitch. (You might want to mark the stopping point with a vanishing marker.) The outside corner will be on your applique. With the needle in the fabric on its left-hand swing, pivot the fabric so the second leg is now vertical and in front of the needle. Turn the handwheel toward you to be sure the next swing of the needle will be lined up squarely with your first row of stitching; then satin stitch the next side.

Satin Stitch Appliqueing the Clean-Cut Corner

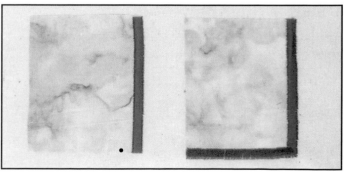

Starting at the right leg of the angle, stitch down to the corner. Leave the needle in the fabric on the left-hand swing. Pivot the fabric on the needle so the second leg is now vertical and in front of the needle. Turn the handwheel toward you until the needle comes out of the fabric; move the fabric to the right so you can bring the needle back down into the same pivoting hole. Continue satin stitching the second leg of the angle.

Tip:

*Satin Stitch Applique Tip from
Donna Wilder,
host of the PBS TV SHOWS
"Sew Creative" and
"Quilt Central",
and founder of
"Free-Spirit"™ Fabrics:*

"Stitch a row of straight stitching around each design prior to satin stitching around edges. This will hold the fabric in position and give you a needle edge to follow, which will make it easier to do the satin stitching. I really enjoy working with Sulky Threads for applique work. Not only do they have a tremendous range of colors, the thread has a beautiful luster that enhances the applique work." --- Donna

Why Do a Computer Applique by Machine?

by Lindee Goodall, co-founder of Cactus Punch®

1. You can make a large impact design in a fraction of the time it takes to do a solid machine embroidery design.

2. Fabric selection can dramatically alter the appearance of the design. Fabric can be patterned, solid, textured, etc.

3. Appliques can be sewn on a wider range of fabrics and often with better results than a solid embroidery. Thick, loopy terry cloth will never poke through an applique even after repeated launderings, which is not the case with embroidery unless a permanent topping has been used.

4. Spend some time thinking about suitable design choices. Did you ever make a garment from a favorite pattern and some wonderful fabric, and the result was anything but wonderful? More than likely the reason was that the fabric was not suitable for that pattern. We have the same situation with embroidery; designs need to be carefully matched to their fabric for successful results. Applique designs are the closest thing to a "universal design solution" that we have.

5. Applique pieces can either be set with Sulky KK 2000 Temporary Spray Adhesive or a fusible web. One of the great things about using KK 2000 is that you can easily reposition an applique several times without leaving any sticky residue behind.

6. Thread choices are endless and fun with Sulky Rayons, Metallics and Cotton Threads being available in such a wide range of colors.

The same computer applique designs are in both pictures, but one uses different thread colors to complement the chosen fabrics while the other uses mostly black. Project on pages 80-86.

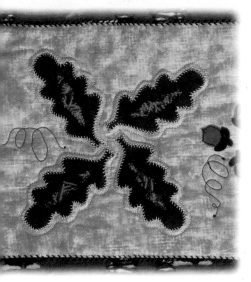

Blanket Stitch by Machine

Sometimes referred to as the Buttonhole Stitch. Most zig-zag machines come with one or more versions of this stitch built-in. The straight stitches should fall directly along the raw edge of the applique without being on top of it. The side stitches will periodically swing into the fabric and back out again. This decorative stitch is used both on raw-edged fabric appliques and those that are fused to the background fabric. The stitch lays over the applique's edge and hides it. Adjust the size of the stitch width and length depending on the size of the applique itself. A smaller, more intricate design will require a short stitch length and narrow width. A larger design will look best when done in a longer stitch length and width. Learning how many stitches your machine takes between each left swing will help you in maneuvering around curves and points; when you reach a point, stop with the needle in the fabric and pivot before stitching another left swing into the fabric.

Close-up of one portion of this Flannel Autumn Table Runner which shows how effective Sulky Cotton 12 wt. Thread can be for Blanket Stitch or Buttonhole Stitched Applique.

Any Sulky Decorative Thread can be used for this stitch. (Use the same color thread in the bobbin.) If a matte look is desired for a more old-country, primitive look, use Sulky 12 wt. Cotton or two strands of Sulky 30 wt. Cotton Threads through a 16/100 needle (reduce the top tension as needed and do practice stitching on a scrap before attempting your project). For a bolder, shinier look, try two strands of Sulky 30 wt. Rayon through a 16/100 needle. Of course, Sulky Metallics, Sliver™ or Holoshimmer™ can also be used, and a 14/90 Metallic Needle is recommended.

The Autumn Table Runner (left) was stitched by Carol Ingram using 2 strands of Sulky 30 wt. Rayon through the machine needle. (Designs and cutting instructions can be found on Pattern Sheet #4.) Choose thread colors that will best show off your applique and fabric. The Pine Cone design is from Carol Ingram's Signature Series Embroidery Card #5,. Holiday Trapunto, by Cactus Punch™.

Below is a close-up from the Daisy May Vest project found on pages 90-93 which shows how effective Invisible Applique with Sulky Polyester Invisible Thread can be.

Invisible Applique by Machine

This technique uses Sulky Polyester Invisible Thread in either smoke for dark fabrics or clear for light fabrics, and a machine blind hem stitch. If your machine doesn't have a blind hem stitch, a zig-zag stitch can be used. For either stitch, on most machines, select a width and length of 1.

Turn under the edges of the fabric applique either with a pin or pointed wooden skewer, or press the edges under using a template; or try the Solvy-Turn Technique (see the Funky Chicken Quilt on page 60). Sulky KK 2000 can also be used to temporarily hold the edges under, as well as holding the whole applique to the background fabric.

When using the blind hem stitch, put the applique edge to the left of the presser foot so the straight stitches fall along the edge of the applique onto the background fabric, not onto the applique itself. When using the zig-zag with the width set at 1, position the fabric so that on the right swing of the needle it enters only the background fabric, directly against the edge of the applique. In both cases, the "bite" or swing of the needle should only catch a few threads of the applique fabric. Adjust the stitch width as needed. It's always a good idea to practice a new stitch technique before attempting it on the real project.

Decorative Stitch Applique by Machine

Generally, when appliqueing with machine decorative stitches, use any of the beautiful Sulky Decorative Threads. Each of the projects in this book will suggest which type of Sulky Thread to use since it will affect the final finished result. Take some time to play with your decorative built-in stitches using Sulky Rayon, Cotton, Metallic and Polyester Threads. Consult pages 3-13 for details on how to get the best results with each type of Sulky Thread.

The heavier Sulky 30 wt. Rayon will give a look of shiny silk, with a fuller fill-in than Sulky 40 wt. Rayon. However, the 40 wt. Rayon tends to be more manageable for a beginner. The Sulky 30 wt. Cotton will give the same fullness as 30 wt. Rayon, but with a matte finish. For some decorative stitch patterns, the Sulky 12 wt. Cotton will give a look of hand-worked crewel embroidery. Sulky Sliver™ and Sulky Holoshimmer™ will give a more reflective, brilliant look than Sulky Original Metallic, which has a nice sparkle.

Just like Satin Stitch Applique, if the fabric has a raw edge, make part of the stitching just cover the raw edge of the applique, with the rest stitching into the applique. However, put the edge of the applique in the center of the stitching for stitches like the Bead or Arrow stitch.

Decorative stitch patterns with one flat edge are also excellent for applique. Keep the flat edge on the edge of the applique's background fabric and the bulk of the stitching on the applique.

Carol Ingram's Tuxedo Vest Project (on pages 94-98) shows off many of the decorative stitches on her Viking Designer 1 Sewing Machine using Sulky Sliver™ Metallic Thread.

Stitched with Sulky 12 wt. Cotton Thread.

Stitched with Sulky 30 wt. Cotton Thread.

"Herky Jerky"™ Free-Motion Applique Stitch

This is a fun-filled way to applique that does not require the precision and pivoting techniques needed for traditional satin stitch applique. Kathleen Parman developed this stress-free way to applique. Kathleen has experimented with many different thread types and prefers the matte finish look of the new Sulky 30 wt. Cotton Thread for her stained glass block designs. Keep following the Bright Ideas Design line of patterns as Kathleen introduces new patterns using her Herky Jerky stitch which provide playing time with the Sulky Rayon Variegateds and Multi-Colors in both 30 wt. and 40 wt., *new* 12 & 30 wt. Cottons, Metallics, and the *new* Holoshimmer™ Threads. Stained Glass Flower instructions are on page 99.

Raw Edged Straight Stitch Applique

This is one of the fastest and easiest forms of applique. A design can range from an extremely detailed one with small pieces, to a simplistic one using fabric prints as design images. The key words here are "raw edged". This means you do not turn the edges under before stitching them, or cover them with a satin stitch. The raw edge look has become a favorite for collage work where many fabrics are fused down using an iron-on fusible web or, for a less stiff feel, sprayed with KK 2000 Temporary Spray Adhesive to hold them in place until random straight stitching is done over the pieces. When washed, the edges of the appliques fray. Any of Sulky's Decorative Threads can be used for this straight stitch technique. (Use the same color thread in the bobbin.) If a matte look is desired for an old-country, primitive look, use Sulky 12 wt. Cotton or two strands of Sulky 30 wt. Cotton (16/100 needle for either); reduce the top tension so that no bobbin thread is showing on top. (Do test stitching.) For a shinier look, try two strands of Sulky 30 wt. Rayon through a 16/100 needle. Of course Sulky Metallics, Sliver™ or Holoshimmer™ can also be used, but only with at least a 14/90 Metallic Needle. Stitch with a lot of different thread types, or only one type, until you get the look and textured feel that you desire.

Another great example of this technique that is also featured in the "Patchwork" Book is this Jacket above made from the reversible Gypsy Jacket Pattern by Maggie Walker. It features fish on one side and parrots on the other side. It was created by the late Loretta Durian who embellished it with Sulky Sliver Metallic on top and Pearl Cotton in the bobbin. Truly a beautiful work of wearable art.

The Liberty Vest, by Joyce Drexler, pictured to the left is featured in the "Patchwork Concepts in Sulky", Book #900B-9, which has step-by-step colored photos and instructions for the raw edge applique techniques used on this vest and more. This technique is great to try with kids. Let them cut out designs from fabric and show them how easy it is to straight stitch over them with Sulky Thread to incorporate into a beautiful pillow or wallhanging that they can be proud of.

You can give a finished look to raw edged applique by couching a cord over the edge using Sulky Thread in an open zig-zag stitch or blanket stitch. Use a Couching Foot for best results - consult your machine manual.

Couched Raw Edge Applique

In the 2001 Sulky Challenge, Lila Suggs, the Grand Prize Winner in the Professional Division for her wallhanging, used a combination of applique stitch techniques including this beautifully couched edge technique. All of her work is simply exquisite.

You can become a winner in the next Sulky Challenge. For details on entering, see the Sulky website: www.sulky.com.

How to Prepare Fabrics for Applique using Sulky Stabilizers

The Foundation – All applique begins with a foundation (fabric, stabilizer, or garment) on which to place the applique design. The foundation needs to be stable before any applique stitching is done. The Sulky **non-woven** stabilizers that are most commonly used to create the necessary stability for applique include:

• *Sulky Tear-Easy™* – A lightweight, temporary tear-away. Place one or more layers under the area to be stitched. When appliqueing is finished, simply tear away each layer separately to avoid distorting or breaking the stitches.

• *Sulky Totally Stable™* – An iron-on stabilizer. One side has a slick coating that will adhere to fabric, the other side feels cloth-like. Place the slick side on the wrong side of the foundation fabric and fuse with an iron. One or more layers may be necessary depending on the weight of the foundation. Tear away excess when project is completed.

• *Sulky Solvy™, Super Solvy™, Ultra Solvy™* and *Paper Solvy™* – Water Soluble Stabilizers. Dissolve in water, scraps saved from other projects to make a liquid stabilizer. (See formulas in packaging.) On washable fabrics, brush or spray it on the foundation, letting it dry to make it stiff enough to handle the applique stitching without puckering. Then, wash it out and rinse well to bring the foundation fabric back to its original texture. Or, use one of them as a topper stabilizer to hold down the nap of fabrics like terry cloth. Secure it in a hoop with the terry cloth (foundation) under it. After applying the appliques, cut or tear excess away from stitching, and save. Submerge project in water to dissolve the rest. Paper Solvy is ideal for running through the copier and making paper pieced and quilting patterns that wash away after being stitched.

• *Soft 'n Sheer™* – A permanent, soft stabilizer used under T-shirts and lightweight sweatshirts, or any stretchy type fabrics. The amount of layers depends on whether or not work is to be appliqued in a hoop; less layers in a hoop, more if not in a hoop. After stitching, trim away excess. The rest remains under the stitching to help support it through washings. It can also be used as the "foundation fabric" when making free-form, embroidered appliques (see pages 148-150 for ornament project).

• *Cut-Away Plus™* – A medium-weight, permanent stabilizer which is also ideal for use as a "foundation fabric". It was used on the Landscapes featured in the Color Theory Section (pattern on Pattern Sheet #3). Also use it in a hoop under stretchy, heavier-weight sweatshirts and outerwear foundations. For non-hoop applications, pin baste or spray Sulky KK 2000 Temporary Adhesive onto material to adhere it to Cut-Away Plus. Ideal for woven or knit fabrics. Use one or more layers as needed. Cut away the excess once stitching is complete.

• *Sulky Sticky +™* – A self-adhesive, temporary tear-away stabilizer that is super easy to use as a hooping aid when doing computerized applique. It provides super stability combined with effortless removal, and it doesn't gum up the machine needle.

Using Sulky Tear-Easy as a Foundation for Stained Glass or Battenburg Lace Applique –

Trace the pattern onto Tear-Easy, or run Tear-Easy through a copier by adhering it to a piece of paper and hand feeding it into the copier. Trace the same pattern onto Totally Stable and cut it apart, using the pieces as templates for cutting the individual fabric patches. Label or number each piece for easy assembly. Iron the pieces onto the right side of the appropriate fabrics. Don't worry about seam allowances since fabrics will be butted, not sewn together and bias tape or Battenburg Tape is applied over the butted-together area of the fabrics.

Using Sulky Sticky as a Template –

Stick two or more layers of Sulky Sticky together and trace your applique pieces onto them. Cut out each piece as a template, adhere them to fabric choices, cut fabric around the template, and pull off the Sticky.

Using Sulky Totally Stable as a Template –

Trace your applique pieces onto Sulky Totally Stable. Iron onto fabrics, then cut out the applique pieces, following the tracing on the stabilizer.

Color Theory 101
for Applique using the Sulky Thread Palette

"The first thing you need to know about color is that nothing is constant or absolute! The influence and impact of any given color changes every time it is put into a new environment." --- Gai Perry, Color from the Heart, published by C&T Publishing (See page 38 for web site).

Color, the how, when, where and how much, is a personal and emotional expression of an individual's artistic eye. Our perceptions of color are instinctive. The eye responds to a visual stimuli that is processed by the brain into many forms of expression and emotion, and it also helps us define space and physical form. An artist can express feeling and mood in a painting, an interior decorator adds comfort and atmosphere to a living area and a fashion designer can cause heads to turn on the runway, all with color. An enormous wealth of color is available to us, and we marvel at the colors of the seasons, or at a beautiful rainbow or sunset. Although it is all around us, we still remain awed by the mystery of color and just how to apply it with harmonious results.

It's no mystery. Some of us have a natural sense for color harmony, but, like anything else, it can be learned, and the principles are fairly simple. When you apply that learned color theory, incorporating your own taste, as seen through your inner eye, you step into the world of designing, be it fashion, painting, home decorating, quilting or textile art. Usually someone who has little or no color theory background stays with something safe like a favorite one-color palette, or something neutral like beige and brown, or they may even venture into a two-color palette if they feel that "pink and green are good together". Often this leaves us unsatisfied with a finished project that may be very nice, but very often is somehow lacking. By knowing a little color theory and how to apply it, your projects will not only reflect your own personal style, but have more impact and visual appeal.

A basic foundation for color theory explores the color wheel and its three primary colors: red, yellow, and blue, plus adding black and white. Remember, this is Basic Color Theory 101 and we're going to keep it simple.

Carol Ingram
Artist, Designer for Sulky of America®, Cactus Punch®, and Fabric Traditions®

Carol is an accomplished artist in the Fine Arts field, including oil painting, pastels and pencil drawing. She has studied art extensively in college and under private instruction from notable national art instructors. Her background brought Carol to a cooperative designing relationship with Cactus Punch, and they have produced seven top-selling computerized machine embroidery "Signature Series" cards from Carol's original artwork. She has also designed an embroidery card for Husqvarna Viking.

In 2001, her first line of fabric, "Snow Follies" was produced by Fabric Traditions.

Her 40 years of sewing experience has provided her with special insight into combining art and textiles into a versatile product.

She presently is a designer and educator for Sulky of America. She has taught at Husqvarna Viking Sewing Conventions, and does free-lance teaching at local sewing stores around Florida. She was a first place winner of the Everyone Loves Sulky Challenge in 1996. She has also contributed many exclusive designs for other Sulky books and presentations for PBS TV sewing programs such as Martha's Sewing Room, Sew Creative, and America Sews with Sue Hausmann.

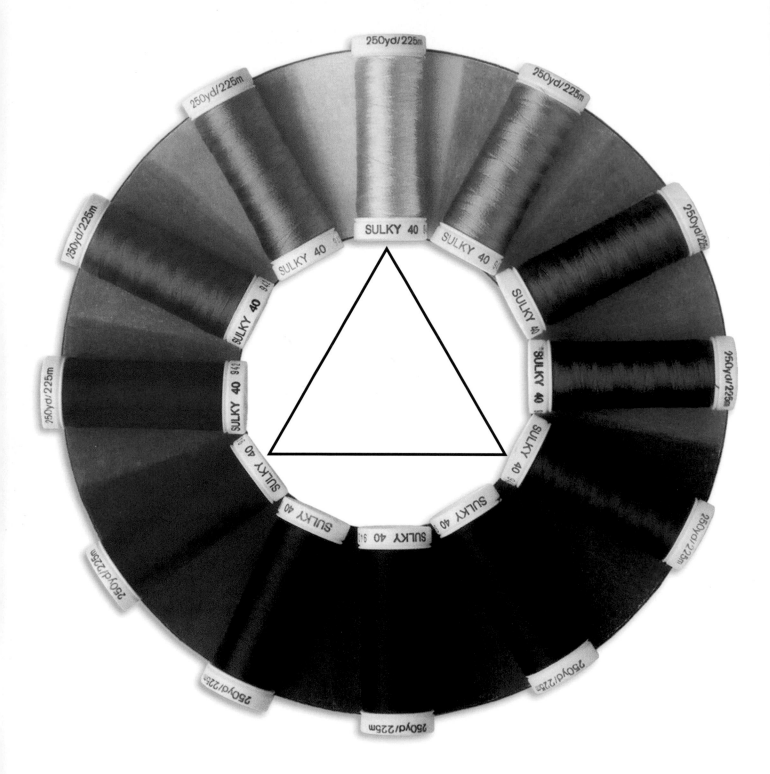

The Sulky Thread Color Wheel

The color wheel is a basic chart used to help those of us struggling with color theory to understand colors, where they belong, and how they relate to each other. By going around the wheel, you can identify the relationships of adjoining colors and, by working across the wheel, identify opposites or complementary colors. On the next 3 pages you will learn how to select the colors that make up this wheel.

See Sources page 164 for ordering a "Rainbow™ Color Wheel" as pictured on page 27.

The Primary Colors – Yellow, Red, and Blue

To the left is an example of a landscape done in very dramatic, primary color fabrics. It features Decorative Applique stitches using Sulky 40 wt. Rayon colors.

Primary and Secondary colors of Sulky 40 wt. Rayon Thread are available in a Sulky "Sampler Box" of 6 spools. Item #942-16.

Below is an example of primary colors used in this outfit by National Sulky Educator, Trish Liden. She enlarged the designs in the print of the skirt to create the appliques.

We start by drawing a basic, equal-sided triangle and a full 360 degree circle around it. By touching the tips of the triangle with the circle, we divide it to place the three primary colors on the wheel. Start by placing the three primary colors at the tips of the triangle. Carol chose yellow at the top, blue at the lower right and red at the lower left. The placement of these colors is academic since they are all relative, as you will soon see when we mix the secondary colors. These colors placed on the wheel should be pure color, meaning they are not mixed with any other color. At this point there are three Primary colors on the wheel.

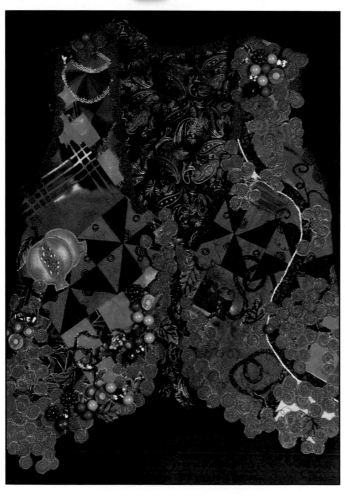

The Secondary Colors – Green, Purple and Orange

Secondary colors are simply an equal mixture of two of the primary colors; that color is placed along the circle, an equal distance between those two primary colors. Yellow and blue, mixed in equal portions with no other color added, makes green, which is placed halfway between yellow and blue. Blue and red, mixed in equal portions with no other color added, makes purple, which is placed halfway between blue and red. Red and yellow, mixed in equal portions with no other color added, makes orange, which is placed halfway between red and yellow. You now have six colors on your color wheel: three primary (red, yellow, blue); and three secondary (green, purple and orange).

Above is an example of an appliqued vest done in secondary colored fabrics by Virgie Fisher shown step-by-step on pages 17-19 of the book, **Embellishing Concepts in Sulky #900B-8.**

The Tertiary Colors

Yellow-Green, Blue-Green, Blue-Violet, Red-Violet, Red-Orange, and Yellow-Orange

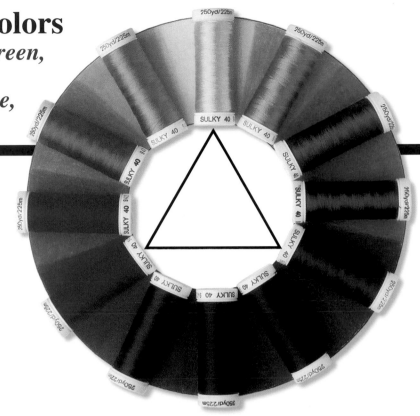

Tertiary colors are created in the same way by mixing equal portions of a primary color with an adjacent secondary color.

Yellow + Green = Yellow-green
placed between yellow and green.

Blue + Green = Blue-green
placed between blue and green.

Blue + Purple = Blue-violet
placed between blue and purple.

Red + Purple = Red-violet
placed between red and purple.

Red + Orange = Red-orange
placed between red and orange.

Yellow + Orange = Yellow-orange
placed between yellow and orange.

All around the drawn circle, you now have twelve colors on your color wheel:

Three Primary
(red, yellow, blue)

Three Secondary
(green, orange, purple)

and **Six Tertiary Colors:**
(yellow-green, blue-green, blue-violet, red-violet, red-orange, yellow-orange)

A true basic color wheel.

The Tertiary Colors of Sulky 40 wt. Rayon are available in a Sulky "Sampler Box" of 12 spools. Item #942-17.

To the right is an example of a landscape done using Tertiary colored fabrics. It incorporates the satin stitch and decorative stitch applique methods featuring the blanket stitch, grass stitch and other decorative stitches using Sulky 40 wt. Rayon colors.

Value - Lightness & Darkness of a Color

Once you are familiar with the placement of colors on the color wheel, it's time to consider the basic principles of color and how to apply them.

The principles of color are common to all media and one generally starts with a personal palette...the color palette that most appeals to your inner eye, and works best for you. From fashion to home decorating to fiberart, we encounter terminology such as value, intensity, contrast, shades, tints and tones. What do all these terms mean...simply stated?

We will start with a <u>pure color</u> - one of the 12 undiluted colors on the color wheel - so called because they have not been lightened with white or darkened with black, and we will create values of these colors.

Look at these examples of VALUE --- the degree of lightness and darkness of one color. Above is a section from a vest by Marilyn Fisher, a Sulky "Sew Exciting Seminar" Educator; below is a watercolor wallhanging by Carol Ingram, designer for Sulky of America.

<u>Value</u> is the degree of lightness and darkness of one color. Value is important in determining how light or how dark you want your project to be. To do this, we must first explore a Gray Scale. Gray is the mixing of black and white in various degrees. A Gray scale starts with pure black and adds white in 10 percent increments, gradating to a pure white; generally it has at least 9 different values.

By using the same mixture principle and applying it to a particular color, you create a <u>Value Scale</u>. Place one of the pure colors, such as pure red, in the middle of your scale. Start by adding black and gradating towards the darkest value, adding black in 10% increments to <u>Shade</u> the red color, making it darker. Then add white, gradating toward the lighter values in 10% increments to <u>Tint</u> the red color, making it lighter.

Above is an example of a color Value Scale that would apply to any color or hue. Values that are far apart on the scale are considered <u>Contrasting</u> or

<u>High Contrast.</u> Applying the principles of a value scale to textiles, we would describe them as light-lights, medium-lights, dark-lights, light-mediums, dark-mediums, light-darks, medium-darks, and dark-darks; this process is used in quilting to make "watercolor" quilts.

Color Palettes
Intensity, Contrast and Proportion

Now that we understand "Tinting and Shading" in a value scale, let's add additional colors to our color wheel. By leaving each pure color on the circle and adding black, working on the outside of the wheel, we shade all the colors darker, adding more colors. Then we add white to each color progressively and lighten them as we progress inward on our color wheel. Depending on how many values of each color chosen, you add considerably to your wheel.

We categorize those colors and refer to these different categories as **COLOR PALETTES.**

You certainly couldn't ask for a larger and more versatile color palette than Sulky offers with 387 rayon colors to choose from.

These color palettes are subject to the interpretation of the artist/designer, and they project personal style and mood. The designer may also maneuver the <u>intensity</u> and <u>contrast</u> of the palette, further strengthening the visual impact of the designs.

Intensity is simply the purity of the color - the color is most intense when it is pure color without another color added to it to either lighten, gray, darken or neutralize it.

Contrast, on the other hand, is combining opposite elements like light and dark values or warm and cool colors. Contrast can also be achieved by using <u>Proportion.</u>

Color proportion guideline: Think of the colors you are assigning to your space as a gallon of your main color, a quart of your supporting colors and an ounce of accent.

Space proportion guideline: Space is more pleasing when it is divided into two-thirds / one-third instead of divided in half. If you are using three colors, reserve 10% of your space for your accent, then divide the remaining portion into one-third/two-thirds. For a four-color combination, divide the one-third portion into one-third/two-thirds.

Remember that the division of space and the colors that fill the space are usually more pleasing when they are not used in equal proportions.

The graphics below and proportion guidelines are used with permission from the Rainbow™ Color Sense brochure, a companion to the Rainbow Pick, Point & Match® Color Selector. See Sources page 164 for ordering the Wheel.

Proportion:
As you look at your color combinations, remember that the division of space and the colors that fill the space are usually more pleasing when they are not used in equal proportion. There are mathematical formulas for determining space and color proportions, however the two statements below will serve as general guidelines.

Color Proportion Guideline:
Think of the colors you are assigning to your space as a gallon of your main color, a quart of your supporting colors and an ounce of accent or spark.

Space Proportion Guidelines:
Space is more pleasing when it it divided into two-thirds/one-third instead of divided in half.

2/3   1/3 divided into 2/3 + 1/3

Black, White & Gray
"The Neutrals"

Black is really the absence of color. In painting, it is added to colors to darken or shade, and it is mixed with white to make grays to tone. Black is very strong and, when placed around a pure color, makes the color more intense and brighter, causing it to appear larger. White, on the other hand, is the presence of all colors. It is light which holds all colors. Sir Isaac Newton, in the seventeenth century, proved the white theory when he passed a stream of light through a prism and it reflected the bands of the color spectrum. The same thing happens in the sky when sunlight passes through tiny droplets of water acting as prisms, creating a magnificent rainbow of color through the sky.

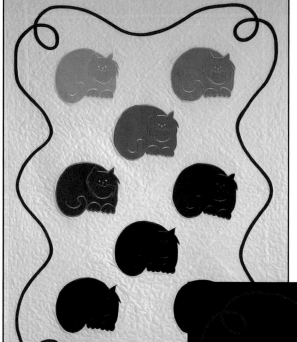

White acts exactly the opposite of black. When placed beside a pure color, it makes the color appear duller and smaller. White mixed with pure color lightens as well as softens and makes colors more pastel. White mixed with black gives us varying shades of gray. White, black and gray will be classified as neutrals as we address the Color Wheel.

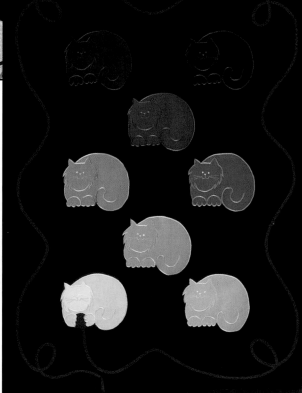

Above and to the right: "Appliqued Cats" A study of the Gray Scale *by Beverly Johnson. See pages 158-160 for directions to make these beautiful cat wallhangings.*

Achromatic colors of Sulky 40 wt. Rayon Thread are available in a Sulky "Sampler Box" of 10 spools. Item #942-09

Earthy Neutrals

A Neutral Palette:

Neutrals are colors made from blacks and whites in mixtures of gray, or complementary mixtures of muddy browns. Shading and tinting changes the value of these neutrals, and the palette then takes on many more colors. Neutrals can either be used entirely by themselves, used only in backgrounds, or added to other color palettes to soften them.

Neutrals add balance to a design. In bolder palettes, they are used to allow the eye to rest and to help the viewer travel visually through the design without confusion. A neutral, earth-toned palette gives you a natural, rich and warm feel. You can create drama within a design by adding one of the two pure complements used to mix the earth tones; for instance, adding bright orange or terra cotta to a neutral brown palette.

"Almost any color can be put into a neutral color scheme if it's so diluted that it becomes non-competitive." - Gai Perry, <u>Color from the Heart</u>.

Above: "Fireworks" by Noriko Nishikawa
from Nishinomiya City, Hyogo, Japan
is an example of Earthy Neutral fabrics that
have been grayed with a dark value of gray.
The hand appliqued Japanese
girl is dimensional.

Above is an example of a landscape done using Earthy Neutral colored fabrics. It features the Blanket Stitch applique using Sulky 40 wt. Rayon colors.

Earthy Neutrals of Sulky 40 wt. Rayon Thread are available in a Sulky "Sampler Box" of 10 spools. Item # 942-10.

Achromatic Palette

An Achromatic Palette:

Achromatic, meaning - without color; anything without an actual color to it such as white or black, or a gray mixture of black or white. For instance, a black and white photograph is Achromatic. Achromatic colors affect the apparent strength of pure colors and are influenced by them when either placed side-by-side or mixed. For our purposes, we are going to classify these in the neutral category. An Achromatic color scheme is safe and easy. Used as white on white, for instance, it can show classic elegance, and it makes an understatement.

A black and white Achromatic palette, with one other color added to it (often called a "kicker"), causes that one color to stand out, indicating strength, boldness and authority, and makes that one added color a focal point of the design.

To the left is an example of a landscape done using the fabrics and Sulky 40 wt. Rayon colors from the Achromatic Palette. It features the satin stitch applique method.

Black to White Sulky 40 wt. Rayon Thread available in a Sulky "Sampler Box" of 10 spools Item # 942-09.

Monochromatic Palette

A Monochromatic Palette: Mono simply means one and Croma means color, one color. A one color palette uses many values of that one color and is safe and easy.

Above is an example of a landscape done using Monochromatic colored fabrics. It features the blanket stitch and decorative stitch applique methods using Sulky 40 wt. Rayon in shades of blue. To the left is an example of a Monochromatic Computer Embroidered Snowglobe (from Carol Ingram's Signature Series # 85 Card) Applique using Sulky 40 wt. Rayon.

Polychromatic Palette

A Polychromatic Palette:

Poly means exhibiting many (chroma) colors. A mixture of all pure colors on the color wheel is exciting, active and stimulating, but sometimes can be distracting and unfocused. The proper balance of dominant and subordinate colors is important or it will not have a focal point, and can be confusing to the eye. Usually you associate a polychromatic scheme with happiness and fun like circus clowns or preschool learning centers. A softer polychromatic palette is often used in landscapes and street scenes, to create a totally different mood or effect. Polychromatic palettes can be a little more challenging, but proper use of balance, contrast and value will make it magical.

To the right is an example of a landscape done using Polychromatic colored fabrics. It features the satin stitch and decorative stitch applique methods using Sulky 40 wt. Rayons in coordinating colors.

An Analogous (Neighboring) Palette

An Analogous Palette:

Having similarity in appearance, sometimes referred to as "neighboring" on the color wheel. Usually three or more consecutive colors that lay side-by-side and are similar in appearance on the color wheel are Analogous (neighboring).

Usually one color is dominant and the others are subordinate in descending grades. By adding value, intensity and contrast, an Analogous palette can create a great deal of impact and mood. It is also a safe and easy palette to work with.

This Analogous Palette of Sulky 40 wt. Rayon Threads are available in a Sulky "Sampler Box" of 10 spools Item # 942-08.

Above: Mary Billow (author Joyce Drexler's mother), models an Analogous, Celtic Cutwork, Appliqued Scarf made by "Sulky Sew Exciting Seminar" educator, Suzy Seed from Houston, TX.

To the left is an example of a landscape done using Analogous colored fabrics and Sulky 40 wt. Rayons. It features the Satin Stitch Applique method.

Complementary Palette

A Complementary Palette:

Consisting of two colors (and shades thereof) directly across from one another on the color wheel; for instance, red and green. Complementary color palettes are very dramatic and daring, and create a lot of visual excitement.

To the right are examples of the "O Canada Quilt" by Doreen Teasdale of Brampton, Ontario, Canada, showing two different renditions of a Complementary Palette. Notice the dramatic effect that the black background has compared to the white. Designs and instructions are on Pattern Sheet #3.

Above is an example of a landscape done using complementary colored fabrics. Featuring the satin and blanket stitch applique methods using Sulky 40 wt. Rayon colors.

Split-Complement Palette

A Split-Complement Palette:

This is a 3 color palette using two colors on either side of the starting complementary color, along with its complementary color on the opposite side of the wheel.

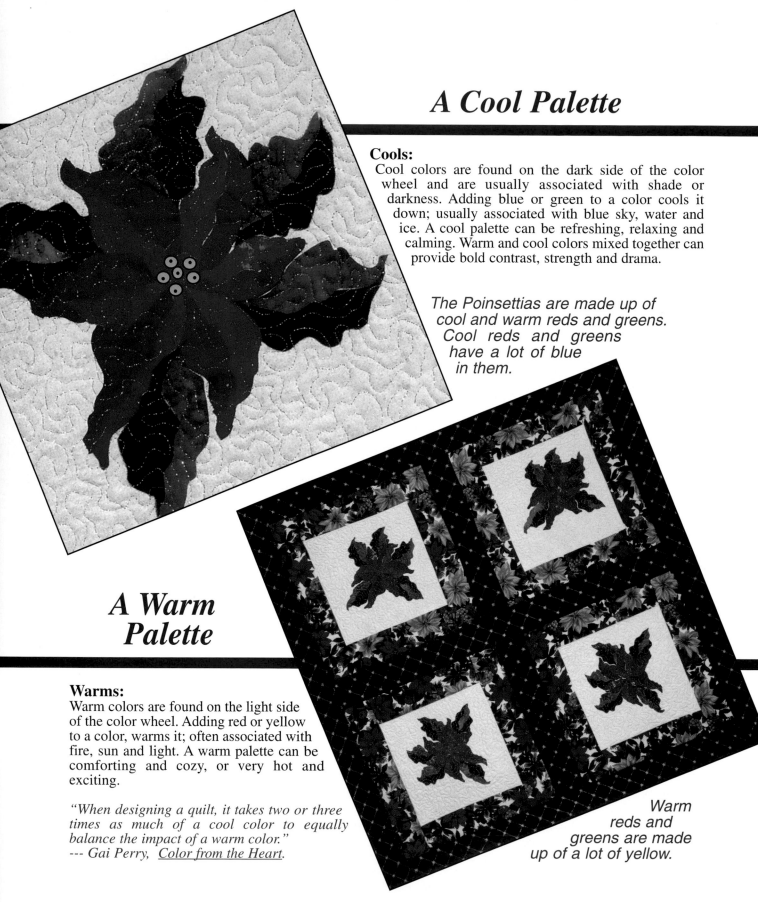

A Cool Palette

Cools:
Cool colors are found on the dark side of the color wheel and are usually associated with shade or darkness. Adding blue or green to a color cools it down; usually associated with blue sky, water and ice. A cool palette can be refreshing, relaxing and calming. Warm and cool colors mixed together can provide bold contrast, strength and drama.

The Poinsettias are made up of cool and warm reds and greens. Cool reds and greens have a lot of blue in them.

A Warm Palette

Warms:
Warm colors are found on the light side of the color wheel. Adding red or yellow to a color, warms it; often associated with fire, sun and light. A warm palette can be comforting and cozy, or very hot and exciting.

"When designing a quilt, it takes two or three times as much of a cool color to equally balance the impact of a warm color."
--- Gai Perry, Color from the Heart.

Warm reds and greens are made up of a lot of yellow.

The Poinsettia design is found on Pattern Sheet #3. It uses the fusible-web, raw-edge applique technique with stippling over it using Sulky Sliver™ Metallic Threads. See pages 102-103 for complete instructions for making the wallhanging.

A Pastel Palette

A Pastel Palette:
Created by tinting a color with white until it is soft and pale. Pastels are always very light, delicate, friendly, and often feminine. When slightly muted with gray, they create a nostalgic and romantic mood. A muted pastel palette is usually used in a Victorian setting. Pure color pastels are often used for wedding, children and baby themes.

This is an example of a landscape done using pastel colored fabrics, but with the gray tones creating a romantic, nostalgic mood. It features a free-motion applique method. This pastel rainbow colored palette of Sulky Original Metallic Threads is available in a Sulky Sampler Box of six spools. Item #142-02.

Some things to consider when creating a textile project:

Color Theory can be kept pretty simple, yet still have a dramatic affect on your creative projects.

1. Starting with your personal inspiration or theme, refer to the basic color wheel to choose your preferred palette of colors - those colors that excite you or make you feel good.
2. Consider the <u>Value</u> of those colors, remembering "Value does all the work and color gets all the credit".
3. Consider the <u>Intensity</u> of those colors. Are they shaded, toned, tinted, pure?
4. <u>Balance</u>: which colors are dominant, intermediate, subordinate, and do you need neutrals for balance?
5. <u>High or Low Contrast</u>: the degree of lightness or darkness - how much of each?
6. Temperature of your color, <u>Warm or Cool</u>? Where and how much?
7. Interest and impact: Do you need or want a <u>Complement or "Kicker"</u>?
8. <u>Proportion:</u> When considering amounts of color for your project, remember equal amounts of color create confusion because there is nowhere for the eye to rest without a focal point.
9. Add <u>Texture</u> and/or <u>Dimension</u> where appropriate.
10. Finally: Review your design, considering your personal color palette and your own inner sense of color. With this simple lesson in color theory you will find your own individual style for working with the colors that you love, adding more pizzazz and interest to your designs.

We are blessed with so many Sulky colors to choose from, our palette is endless and unlimited.

Please read these tips before you begin any of the applique and quilting projects.

IF YOU PRE-WASH YOUR FABRICS -
Be sure to press and spray with Magic Sizing™ to make them easier to handle. Pre-washing is a great idea for any hand-dyed or bali prints to remove any excess dye that might remain.

CUTTING -
Treat yourself to a new blade in your rotary cutter. Having a good cut will reflect in the accuracy of your overall construction. When beginning to cut using your rotary cutter, mat and quilter's ruler, first make a slight cut backwards at the beginning of the cut. Having your pinkie off the ruler and on the table (opposite cutting edge) will help stabilize the ruler. Stagger strips when cutting multiple layers. Square them up with the lines on the ruler. Always cut off selvage edges.

SEWING THREAD -
Use either new Sulky 30 wt. Cotton, poly/cotton, or a good quality 100% polyester machine sewing thread, off-white or cream for relatively light colored fabrics, gray for medium toned fabrics, and brown for dark fabrics.

By pressing seams to the side, stitching will not show if your machine tension is set correctly, and there will be less stress on the seam thread.

MAKE SURE YOU ARE USING AN ACCURATE 1/4" SEAM ALLOWANCE THROUGHOUT THE PROJECT -
Measure your very first seam to be positive it is exactly 1/4", especially when making the Trip Around the World Quilts as background for Trapunto Applique. Most machines today have an accurate 1/4" foot available either with the machine or as an accessory. With some machines it is possible to use the edge of the presser foot as a 1/4" guide. However, to be sure, stitch some sample seams using scrap fabric, and measure the seam allowance carefully. If you have a computerized machine, there is usually an easy way to set the machine for an exact 1/4" seam by changing the needle position.

USE THE SAME SEWING MACHINE AND FOOT -
To ensure that the seam allowances stay a true and uniform 1/4", use the same machine and foot when piecing the blocks for any quilt.

MATCHING SEAMS -
Use extra-long quilting straight pins or silk pins to help match seams. Simply put the pin point straight through the first layer seam joint, then carefully look to see that the point again penetrates at the second layer seam joint that you are trying to match. Then, when you penetrate the layers the second time, repeat the procedure so that the pin repeats its penetration in the seam line for both layers. It's a snap - and also a sure thing!

SECURING THREADS -
You will **not** need to backstitch at the beginning and ending of pieced strips and squares since these edges will become seam allowances as you continue to cut and piece. However, handle sewn pieces carefully so stitching does not come undone. Since it is always best to lock off your first and last stitch, if you have a relatively new machine, it probably has a single pattern button or a lock stitch button which you can use to lock off your first and last stitch. That does not mean back stitch. Leave tails long and thread them through a hand needle. Bury the threads in between the top and bottom layers of the quilt.

PRESS ALL SEAM ALLOWANCES -
Press all seams to one side toward darkest fabric because seams might show through light-colored fabric when batting and backing are placed behind the face of the quilt.

Unless instructed to do so, do not press any seams open. To avoid distorting the fabric shape when pressing seams, press only (*do not slide the iron*). Press the wrong side first, then the right side.

- **No steam.**
- **Press first from the back, setting the seam.**
- **Press again from the front.**

MOST USED MACHINE QUILTING STITCHES -
"Stitching in the Ditch" - This is one of the most basic of quilting stitches by machine. The "ditch" is actually the seam line between pieces, blocks, sashing and borders. Use the hand wheel to manually lower the needle into the seam line. Always tie on or anchor your stitches. Then straight stitch along the lower side of the seam line (the one that doesn't have the seam allowances pressed toward it). When crossing a seam intersection, the seam allowance may shift to the opposite side. Simply follow along whichever side doesn't have the seam allowance. Usually stitched with Sulky Invisible Thread - Clear for light-colored fabrics and Smoke for dark fabrics. *Experiment with stitching in the ditch using Sulky Metallic or Sliver Thread. It really gives depth to the block.*

"Crosshatch Stitching" - A grid created by making one set of parallel lines intersect perpendicularly with another set of parallel lines. Use a Quilter's Ruler and rolling chalk marker to draw a diagonal line, usually in the center or from corner to corner of either a block, sashing or border. Use a quilt guide to space the grid, or you can draw it out. Tie on and tie off at the beginning and end of each row of stitching. To better show off your stitching, use a slightly longer stitch length (3.0 or more) and heavier Sulky 30 wt. thread. Consider using decorative stitches, twin-needles and Sulky Variegated and Multi-Colors.

"Stipple (tight); Meandering or Serpentine (loose)" - Set up your machine for "Free-Motion" (see page 58). Use a machine embroidery hoop and/or a darning foot on the machine. Guide the quilt smoothly, making puzzle shapes that are s-shaped curves. Try to keep the stitches looking uniform in stitch length by developing a rhythm between the speed of the machine and movement of the quilt top. Generally, stitching lines will not cross over each other. Stippling lines generally are no more than 1/8" to 1/4" apart, while Meandering is a more loosely spaced stitch.

"Echo Quilting" - A line of stitching that repeats the shape once or in multiples. It can be done "Free-Motion" or machine fed. (See Stippling above and page 58 for free-motion set-up.) If machine fed, use either a clear foot, walking foot or even-feed foot, and a 3.0 straight stitch length; stitch consistently 1/8" or 1/4" away from the seam line of the pieces that make up the blocks or appliqued design. Start your stitching on a smooth edge, not at a point. Always tie on and tie off.

Blanche Young

Dalene Young Stone

Easy Throw or Baby-Size Quilt
Trip Around the World "Baby Sunshine and Shadow"

Authors of the book:
"Tradition with a Twist"
for C & T Publishing

Blanche: *After viewing a quilt made by Blanche, many people have commented on the ability she has to put fabrics and colors together to produce such beautiful creations. Yet, Blanche has never had any formal education in color - she just enjoys the aspects of blending and mixing hues and patterns. Blanche's interest in color began at an early age from watching her father mix paint. Being the local wallpaper hanger and painter, he would stir, add pigment, and explain what the results would be. From her mother, Blanche learned how the careful arrangement of colors in their large flower garden would enhance each other. At age 13, Blanche made her first quilt - a Sunbonnet Sue - using fabrics from a scrap bag. Through the years, Blanche has made hundreds of quilts. Had she known then what she knows today, Blanche vows that her children would not have been allowed to jump on their beds - on the quilts, of course!*

Dalene: *As the youngest of Blanche's daughters, Dalene has always had sewing and fabrics as part of her life. Dalene remembers sharing a bedroom with a sewing machine, and many nights being lulled to sleep by the hum of the machine as her mother worked. At age 13, Dalene received her first sewing machine (although at the time she secretly wished the box contained a stereo) and she made her first quilt - a Lone Star - when she was 16. Today, Dalene machine quilts over 125 quilts a year, in addition to teaching at quilt guilds and shops around the country.*

42" x 54" without Borders.
As featured in their book, *Tradition with a Twist*.

37

Project Overview

The following instructions are taken from the book, **Tradition with a Twist** with permission granted by C&T Publishing.

The instructions for each quilt begins with the cut strips being sewn into strip sets, and then the strip sets being cut into sections. The sections are then sewn into units the width of the quilt to complete the quilt top.

Following the basic construction techniques by Blanche and Dalene you will find quilts that have been appliqued (see pages 43-53) with original paintings by Carol Ingram. You can find the patterns on the Pattern Sheets in the back of this book.

Look for Blanche and Dalene's book at Quilt, Fabric and Book Stores or order directly from:
C&T Publishing
1651 Challenge Dr.
Concord, CA 94520
1-800-284-1114 US
1-925-677-0377

Visit their Web Site:
http://www.ctpub.com
for more information.

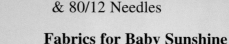

✀ Sewing Machine with 1/4" Foot & 80/12 Needles

Fabrics for Baby Sunshine and Shadow

✀ 5/8 yard each of six fabrics ranging in value from Fabric 1, the lightest, to Fabric 6, the darkest. Cut each color into 2-1/2" x 42-45" strips
✀ 1/4 yard for Inner Borders
✀ 1/2 yard for Outer Borders
✀ 1/2 yard for Binding
✀ 3 yards for Backing
✀ Iron, Pressing Surface
✀ Quilter's Rulers - 4" & 6" widths
✀ Rotary Cutter with sharp blade
✀ Cutting Mat at least 20" x 24"
✀ Small Scissors or Clippers
✀ Cotton or cotton-covered poly thread in a medium shade of the project's main color
✀ Sulky thread of choice for quilting
✀ Sulky KK 2000 Temporary Spray Adhesive for basting quilt

1 Cutting Accurate 2-1/2" x 42-45" Strips

Cutting accurate and straight strips is a very critical step when creating these quilts --- critical but not difficult. To begin cutting strips, work with a length of fabric that fits your mat. Press any wrinkles from the fabric. Then fold the fabric in half, selvage to selvage, and lay it on your cutting mat. Fold a second time, if needed, to fit your mat. The selvages must be kept even (fig. 1). Keep the fabric flat without ruffles or waves along the fold. Line up the folded edge of the fabric that's closest to you, along a permanent inch mark on your cutting mat. Lay your ruler at a right angle to the inch mark, at the right end of your fabric, and align the long edge of your ruler with a vertical inch line on your mat (fig. 2, page 39). As you cut, hold your rotary cutter so the handle is tilted slightly away from your ruler and the blade points toward the ruler at a very slight angle.

If you are left-handed, reverse the left and right instuctions. Your fabric should now have a squared end.

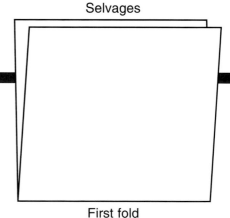

Selvages

First fold

First fold and selvages

Fig. 1   Second fold

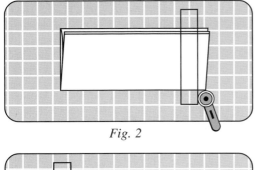

Fig. 2

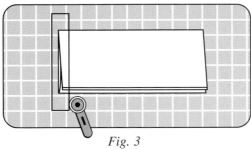

Fig. 3

Carefully turn your cutting mat, with the fabric still on it, so the straight edge is now to your left. Lay your ruler on the left end of the fabric (fig 3) and measure the width of the strip needed through the ruler. Hold the ruler with your left hand and cut with your right hand. Notice that the strip you will cut will be under your ruler.

To check to be sure you are cutting straight strips, open the first strip and lay it on the table. It should have straight cut edges without any slight angle (fig 4). After cutting several strips, you may need to square up your fabric again.

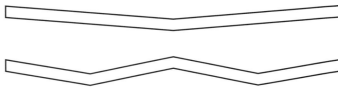

Fig. 4

Seam Allowances 2

All of the seams for the quilts in this book call for a "scant" 1/4" seam allowance because a "full" 1/4" seam allowance leaves the squares a bit smaller than the full finished size. Think of a scant 1/4" allowance as 1/4", less one thread width. To check your scant seam allowance, we recommend the following test: Cut three strips of fabric to measure 1-1/2" x 6". Sew the strips together along the long edges and press the seam allowances away from the center strip. Now, measure across the three strips. This measurement should be 3-1/2" from the raw edge to the raw edge. If your strip set measures more than 3-1/2", try again using larger seams. If it measures less than 3-1/2", try again using smaller seams. The width of your seam allowances can make all the difference in the final result of your piecing. Almost all quiltmakers use a 1/4" seam allowance. While this is a very important point, a **consistent** seam allowance is just as important. We stress the importance of a consistent seam allowance as well as a scant 1/4" seam allowance. Use a seam guide that stays secure and will not move, or try a 1/4" seam allowance foot.

Sewing the Strip Sets 3

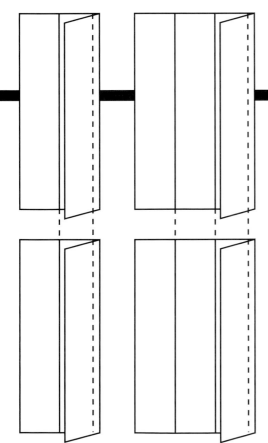

Fig. 5

Strip sets are merely groups of strips sewn together in a predetermined order. When sewing the strip sets, always start with the top strip of each set. Keep track of this top strip by placing a safety pin in its far left-hand corner. To sew the strips together, place the first strip face up on your machine, then place the second strip face down on the first, matching the top selvages. Sew, using a scant 1/4" seam allowance. Let your machine feed the fabric through. (It is unlikely that the selvages at the end of the strips will come out even, so don't let this worry you --- they will be trimmed off later.)

To chain piece the strip sets (Fig. 5), do not cut your threads after sewing the first two strip sets together. Sew past the strip set ends, then place the first and second strips of the next strip set under your machine's foot. (You may have to lift your presser foot to ease the strips under the foot until the feed dog catches the fabric.) Leave the threads intact between the strip sets. After joining all of the first and second strips, start back at the first strip set. Open the two strips and place the third strip face down on the second strip. Stitch together, matching the edges. Add all of the third strips in each set. Continue in this manner, adding all of the needed strips in each strip set. After the strip sets are sewn, cut the threads between the sets.

4

Pressing the Strip Sets

Press the seam allowances in the direction of the even-numbered fabrics in each strip set. Press first from the wrong side of the strips, then press from the right side to remove any pleats that may be along the seam lines. Do not use steam or drag the iron because that can stretch and distort your strip sets.

Stack and Cut the Strip Sets into 2-1/2" Sections

Now that the strip sets are sewn and pressed, they need to be cut into sections of 2-1/2". You can cut one strip set at a time by aligning the strip on your cutting mat, using a horizontal inch line, and then squaring off the end as you did when cutting the strips (Fig. 6). (Then you can cut each section at the 2-1/2" increment.) But, it is much more time efficient to stack and cut several strip sets at once.

To stack the strip sets (Fig. 7), lay the first strip face down on the mat, aligning the long edge along a horizontal inch line on your mat. Lay the second strip set face down upon the first, staggering the second strip approximately 1/8" higher than the first. This will distribute the seam allowances for ease in cutting multiple strips. Stack as many strips as you are comfortable with and that can be cut accurately at one time. Then square up the right end of the strip sets in the same manner as you squared up the fabric when cutting the strips.

Tip: It is helpful to keep one or two of the inch markings on your ruler aligned with one or two of the seam lines in the strip set.

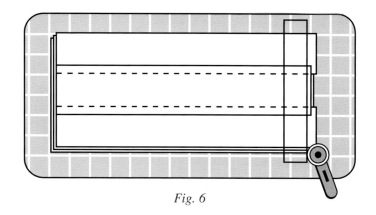

Fig. 6

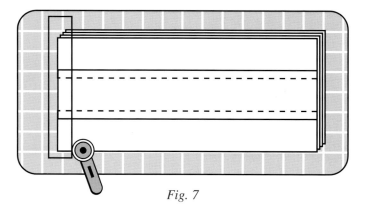

Fig. 7

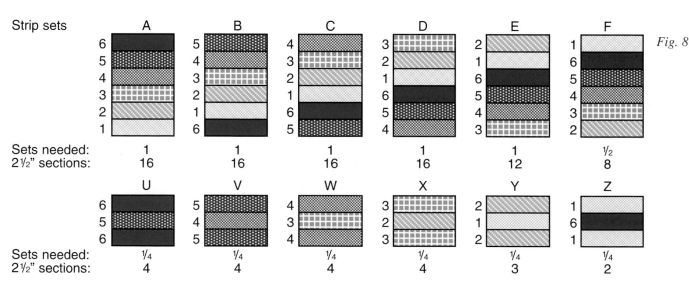

Fig. 8

Strip sets	A	B	C	D	E	F
	6	5	4	3	2	1
	5	4	3	2	1	6
	4	3	2	1	6	5
	3	2	1	6	5	4
	2	1	6	5	4	3
	1	6	5	4	3	2
Sets needed:	1	1	1	1	1	½
2½" sections:	16	16	16	16	12	8

	U	V	W	X	Y	Z
	6	5	4	3	2	1
	5	4	3	2	1	6
	6	5	4	3	2	1
Sets needed:	¼	¼	¼	¼	¼	¼
2½" sections:	4	4	4	4	3	2

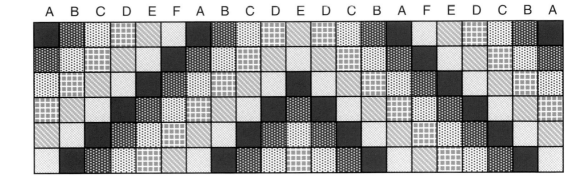

Unit I
Make four

A B C D E F A B C D E D C B A F E D C B A

Unit II
Make one

U V W X Y Z U V W X Y X W V U Z Y X W V U

Fig. 9

The Baby Sunshine and Shadow Quilt is made of five units that span the width of the quilt. There are four of Unit I and one of Unit II (Fig. 9). Two of Unit I are joined to form the top and bottom of the quilt.

Now that all of the sections are stacked, you can begin sewing the main units together. Use chain piecing to facilitate construction of Unit I. Take the first section of the unit (section A) and lay it face up on your machine. Take the next section (which will be the second section of the unit or section B) and place it face down on top of the first section. Sew these two sections together.

Without clipping your threads, repeat this step with the three remaining sections. Continue adding the sections to each main unit. Press the seam allowances as directed in the piecing instructions.

This is a king-size quilt pieced by Sharon Stokes and quilted by Evelyn Howard on a long-arm machine with Sulky 30 wt. Rayon variegated thread using these same techniques, only adding more units to make the size. (See the book, Tradition with a Twist, for instructions to make a bedsize Trip Around the World.)

7   Press the Units

Press the seams after the sections are sewn together. Press the seams of Unit II and two of Unit I toward the left. Press the seams of the two remaining Unit I's toward the right.

8   Sew the Units together

Lay the units together so the pressed seam allowances will nest together at each seam line. Sew the units together in the order shown to the right.

9   Add Borders

First you need to determine the actual size of your quilt top. Before measuring, press the quilt top to make sure it is free from any creases and wrinkles. To measure, lay the quilt flat on a floor or table. For an accurate measurement, **do not** measure along the edges of the quilt, since they are easily stretched. Instead, measure through the center of the quilt from the top edge to the bottom edge for the length, and measure through the center of the quilt, from side to side, for the width. **Based on these measurements, cut 4-1/2" wide strips for a 4" finished border.**

If you are adding two or more borders, be sure to allow for the widths of all preceding borders in your measurements when figuring the yardage of the second or third.

Cut the number of strips needed for the border, trim off the selvages and seam them together, end to end or at right angles, with a 1/4" seam allowance. Press the

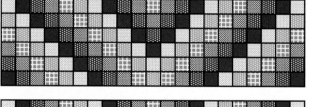

Unit I

Unit I

Unit II

Unit I upside down

Unit I upside down

seams open. From this long piece, cut the border lengths needed. Fold each border strip in half and finger press a crease, or put a pin at the fold. Find the center of the quilt side. With right sides together and the edges even, pin the centers of the border and the centers of the quilt side together. Pin the ends of the border to the corner of the quilt. Next, pin between the existing pins and distribute any fullness over the length of the quilt. Sew on the border using a 1/4" seam allowance. Press the seam toward the border. Add the other side border in the same manner. Before cutting the top and bottom borders to length, you must allow the extra width of the side borders. To your quilt width, add the width of the border twice, less 1" for seam allowances.

10   Quilt & Bind

Quilting: A simple straight line quilting, either in the ditch or at a diagonal line, can be accomplished easily by either hand or machine using a medium stitch length. Many of the Painted, Appliqued Trips were quilted with Sulky 30 wt. Rayon Variegated, but Sulky Cotton or Sulky Metallics could also be used. **Binding:** Since the edges of a quilt receive the most wear and tear, we recommend a double folded binding for finishing the quilts. **Cut a 2-1/2" strip for a finished 1/2" binding. Refer to either of the books <u>Tradition with a Twist</u> or <u>Sulky Secrets to Successful Quilting</u> for more information.**

Trapunto, Appliqued Trip Quilts
Featuring Fabric Print Cut-outs and Hand-Painted Designs

"Cat Print Side Trip" designed by Patti Lee; "Topiary Tree Trip" designed by Joyce Drexler; both were quilted by Evelyn Howard. "Bunny & Birdhouse Side Trip" designed by Carol Ingram and quilted by Marilyn Badger. All three were quilted on a long-arm quilting machine. "Halloween Trip" designed and quilted by Patti Lee. All Fabric Paintings by Carol Ingram.

Patti Lee and Rocco
Director of Consumer Relations and Creative Assistant

Patti Lee has been involved with Speed Stitch and Sulky of America first as a volunteer, then working part-time, and now on a full-time basis since both Companies were formed some 20 years ago. She is currently Consumer Relations Director for Sulky of America. She was a National Instructor for Speed Stitch and an active participant in all nine of their annual S.M.A.R.T. Events. She has also worked in retail sewing machine and fabric stores. In addition to being a contributor to several "Concepts in Sulky" books, she also acts as Joyce Drexler's Creative Assistant and best friend.

Rocco is Patti's newest Assistant. He is only a kitten but he loves to take down all the notes on Patti's bulletin board on a daily, if not hourly basis. He's interested in everything Patti does,

Credits: *"Cat Print Side Trip"* by Patti Lee, features parts of a wallhanging print by Springs Industries. *A variety of wallhanging-size fabric prints can be used for applique themes. Springs' coordinates were used along with fabrics by Moda, M&M Fabrics, Hoffman Fabrics, and Maywood Studio. Quilted by Evelyn Howard using the new* **Sulky 30 wt. Cotton Thread** *on a Long-Arm Quilting Machine.*

Project Overview

The full-size patterns for the painted designs are on pattern sheets #1 and #4. If you do not want to paint the designs, but would like to substitute fabric applique instead, be creative and go for it! However, no special instructions are included to do so.

Even if you have never painted before, we feel the designs are basic enough that even a beginner can be successful with little effort! So branch out and try a new technique. They are gorgeous!

But, if you are not that adventuresome, look for pre-printed wallhanging prints like the cat print shown on page 43. Some really beautiful prints are available with adult motifs that are suitable for any decor or room - not just for children's rooms anymore! Try it - it's easy!

> **You can substitute a purchased fabric print in place of painted motifs if desired. Basic Painting Instructions begin on page 46. Follow the simple instructions on pages 48 and 49 for Trapunto Applique, and the basic assembly instructions below for the "Side Trip" quilts.**

What You Will Need:

- ✂ Sewing Machine
    with 1/4" Foot & 80/12 Needles
- ✂ YLI Wash-Away Thread
- ✂ Sulky Polyester White Bobbin Thread
- ✂ Sulky Threads - for quilting
    See each motif for specific type and color
- ✂ Sulky Polyester Invisible Thread
- ✂ **Fabrics for Quilted Backgrounds**
    See page 38.
- ✂ Low-Loft Batting for Quilt
- ✂ High-Loft Batting for Trapunto
- ✂ Iron, Pressing Surface
- ✂ Quilter's Rulers - 4" and 6" widths
- ✂ Rotary Cutter with sharp blade
- ✂ Cutting Mat at least 20" x 24"
- ✂ Small Scissors or Clippers
- ✂ **Fabric Paints & Supplies:**
    Jo Sonja's Artist's Gouache™
        Fabric Paints (matte finish)
    & Fabric Medium
    (See Sources on page 164)
    • High-count muslin or Dyer's Cloth
        washed, dried and pressed
    • Brushes in Various sizes -
        Boar Bristle/Soft Acrylic/Liners
    • Plastic Paint Palette
    • #2 Lead Pencil
    • Sulky Sticky Stabilizer - *Purchased by the yard off of a bolt so there are no creases - see the pattern for amount needed.*

"Side Trip" Instructions

Refer to the Basic Instructions for making the throw or baby size quilt on pages 37-42. From the basic 5 "Units" from the original Trip Around the World Quilt, assemble the units following the photo to the left for a "Side Trip". Join three "Unit 1's" together. Then sew "Unit 2" to these, with a final "Unit 1" flipped in the opposite direction of the first three "Unit 1's".

Unit 1   +   Unit 1   +   Unit 1   + Unit 2 + Unit 1 flipped

*Credits: **"Halloween Trip"** features fabrics from M&M Fabrics and Moda.*
Quilted by Patti Lee with Sulky 30 wt. Rayon Thread Multi-Color #2245.
Finished size: 50" x 60"

Read These Basic Instructions for all Fabric Paintings:

Basewash the area to be painted using a "fabric medium mixture" of fabric medium and water at a 1:1 ratio. Stay within the pencil line drawing. If the medium bleeds outside the drawn area, the mixture has too much water. When applying "fabric medium mixture" as a basewash, only do small areas so they will not dry before you have blended colors into them. Mix your chosen base color paint with the "fabric medium mixture" at a 1:1 ratio before applying to fabric; always cover the medium painted area with a light wash of this mixture.

Next, mix each of your shading colors at a 1:1 ratio with the "fabric medium mixture" and apply. Finally, use the detail colors to add the details. The fabric medium used for textiles converts the acrylic gouache to a "controlable" textile paint. Proper paint-to-medium mixture ratio helps keep the paint from running, and also helps produce soft and sharp lines in your work.

The paint, mixed at the 1:1 ratio to the "fabric medium mixture", will adequately penetrate the fabric and give that "painterly" look, but still maintain a soft hand or feel to your quilts or garments. If the paint is too thick when applied, it will lay on top of the fabric and not penetrate it, leaving the fabric stiff.

Set Up for Painting *2*

1. Wash, dry and iron the muslin or Dyer's Cloth.
   See Pattern Sheet for size needed for each design.
2. Measure and cut Sulky Sticky to each design size.
3. Remove paper backing from the Sticky and apply to the wrong side of the fabric.
4. With pattern or the preliminary drawing as a guide, use a #2 pencil to trace the outline and detail lines only of the design onto the muslin or Dyer's Cloth, but no shading.
5. Squeeze small amounts of the paints needed onto the plastic palette.
6. Prepare fabric medium mixture in a small container, mixing at a 1:1 ratio - water and medium.

Hint: If you are left-handed, always begin drawing and painting from the far right to the left so you do not drag your hand or arm into the paint. If some paints bleed outside the lines of the drawing, don't worry. You will be trimming the fabric to within 3/4" of the design, and turning under any irregular outside edges prior to appliqueing it onto a quilt or garment, and any bleeding will not show.

Halloween Painting Instructions: *3*

1. *Leaves:*
   Basewash with Yellow Oxide; shade with Green Oxide and Norwegian Orange; paint shadows and lines with Raw Umber.
2. *Pumpkin:*
   Basewash with Norwegian Orange; shadow in veins with mixture of Burnt Sienna and Norwegian Orange. Do details in the shadows and lines with Raw Umber and Carbon Black; do the facial features in Black once the pumpkin has dried.

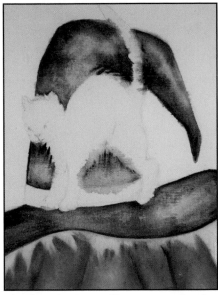
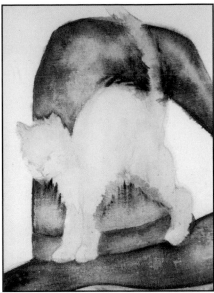

Apply paint in small amounts mixed equally at a 1:1 ratio with fabric medium mixture. Colors are as follows: *Straw under Hat:* Basewash with Yellow Light; details with Raw Umber and Yellow Oxide. *Hat:* Basewash with Carbon Black, light to dark. *Hatband:* Paint with Green Oxide and a lighter shade of Green Oxide mixed with Titanium White. *Cat:* Basewash with Turner's Yellow; shade with Burnt Sienna and Raw Umber and highlight with Titanium White and Smoke Pearl (tail, face, paws, chest fur). *Ghost:* Basewash with Smoke Pearl; shade with Raw Umber and highlight with Titanium White. Paint the eyes and mouth with Carbon Black once ghost is dry.

Topiary Tree

The closeup to the left shows the detail of the free-motion stitching using Sulky 30 wt. Variegated Rayon Thread #2128 Vari-Willow Greens for the leaves and #2102 Vari-Roses for the flowers.

The variations in the color intensity really add a lot of interest and dimension to the overall design.

The leaves were extended with stitching onto the patchwork background to blend them together.

Find this fanciful Topiary Tree Design, with painting instructions and paint colors, on Pattern Sheet #4.

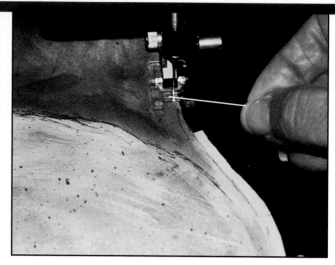

(If using a purchased fabric print, skip down to #3.)

1. Once the painting is finished, remove the Sulky Sticky Stabilizer from the back.
2. Heat-set the painting by pressing from the back with an iron and a press cloth. (The press cloth protects your iron from any stabilizer residue that may remain because of it getting wet by the paint solution.)
3. Trim around the outside edges of the design, leaving approximately a 5/8" seam allowance.
4. Clip into this seam allowance using small, sharp, pointed scissors. Make more cuts closer together where there are more curves, and further apart where the design becomes straighter.
5. Spray the back of the painted applique or fabric print with Sulky KK 2000 Temporary Spray Adhesive and position it on your quilt, wallhanging or garment (henceforth called quilt).
6. Once you are happy with the positioning, pin around the edges.
7. Thread the top with Sulky Polyester Clear Invisible Thread, and the bobbin with regular sewing thread that matches the quilt. Use a very small width and length zig-zag to stitch around the outside edge of the applique, turning under as you go with either a pin, tailor's awl, stiletto or a wooden skewer. Stitch around the entire applique.

> **Tip:**
>
> *Try trimming with "pinking" scissors or a pinking rotary blade cutter, leaving a 1/4" to 3/8" seam allowance. Clip into curves a little more if needed to turn the seam allowance under smoothly.*

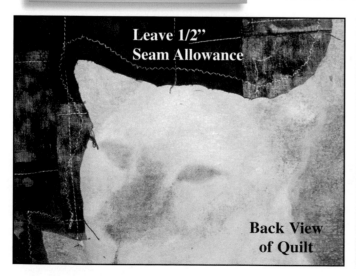

Leave 1/2"
Seam Allowance

Back View
of Quilt

8. From the back of the quilt, use an applique scissors to **VERY CAREFULLY** trim away the portion of the quilt <u>inside the applique design,</u> to within 1/2" of the zig-zag stitching line. This reduces the bulk behind the applique for the trapunto. On the wrong side of the quilt, spray KK 2000 over the backside of the applique, and place a piece of high-loft polyester batting over it (large enough to cover the applique and extend 1" past the edges). Smooth as needed. Pin in several places in the center area of the trapunto.

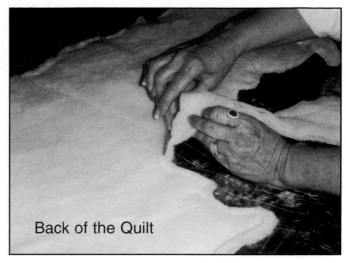

Back of the Quilt

9. Thread the top with a wash-away basting thread, and the bobbin with Sulky Polyester White Bobbin Thread. Set up the machine for free-motion work. With the right side up, free-motion straight stitch around the entire edge of the painted design or fabric print. This stitching does not have to be perfect because it only holds the batting in position during the quilting process, and then is dissolved away with a mist of water.

10. Turn the quilt over to the wrong side and use an applique scissors to trim away the excess batting from around the design. Trim very close to the stitching, leaving batting only behind the painted design or fabric print. Remove pins.

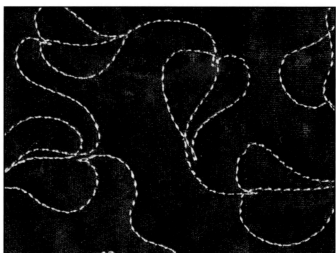

11. Make your quilt "sandwich". With the right side up, use Sulky Polyester Invisible Thread in both the top and bobbin to free-motion straight stitch around the outside edge of the painted or fabric print applique. Quilt the entire quilt in your preferred method, avoiding the painted or fabric print trapunto design areas.

12. To bring out the dimension of the trapuntoed design, use Sulky Rayon colors of your choice to stitch accent lines where appropriate to your design.

13. Optional: Add extra embellishments like the 3-D leaves on the lioness or simple straight-stitched leaves on the Topiary Tree.

14. Bind the quilt and add a hanger on the back, if desired.

Credits: **"Bunny & Bird House Side Trip"** featuring fabrics by Hoffman, and Quilter's Sateen by RJR Fabrics and the beautiful, painted trapunto applique by Carol Ingram, as seen on the front cover of this book. Quilted on a long-arm machine by Marilyn Badger using Sulky Sliver Metallic #8040 Opalescent.

Full-size design patterns and painting instructions can be found on Pattern Sheet #1 in the envelope in the back of this book.

*Credits: "**Topiary Tree**" designed by **Joyce Drexler & Carol Ingram** features fabrics from Robert Kaufman,*
Maywood Fabrics, Hoffman and Benartex.
Quilted by Evelyn Howard on a long-arm machine
on the diagonal, with an "X" design, using Sulky 30 wt. Multi-Color Rayon Thread #2257.
Finished size: 52" x 66"

Short Trip Quilt
Part of the Sulky
"Sew Exciting"™ Seminar 6

Designed by Patti Lee and Carol Ingram

Smiling Sulky National Educators: Top Photo starting at the back row, left to right: Evelyn Howard, Marilyn Fisher, Linda Simmons, Trish Liden, Marilyn Gatz, and Pat Rogers. Center row: Yvonne Perez-Collins, Bev Johnson, Ellen Osten and Patti Lee. Front row: Patsy Shields, Pat Welch, Carol Ingram, and Suzy Seed. Not pictured: Sue Moats, Louise Baird and Joyce Drexler.

Photo to the right - The inspiration for this project was this beautiful watercolor quilt designed by Carol Ingram for her daughter Michelle Burt (pictured here) of Orlando, FL. Carol added depth and interest to this dimensional artwork by appliqueing a water lily, dragon fly and cattails. For more on making Water Color Quilts, see "Sulky Secrets to Successful Quilting" Book 900B-13 by Joyce Drexler.

2 "Short Trip" Layouts

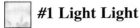 #1 Light Light    #4 Dark Medium

 #2 Dark Light   #5 Light Dark

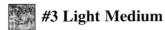 #3 Light Medium   #6 Dark Dark

Cut 6 strips 2" x 45". Sew them into Strip Sets:
  Set 1 - Color #1, #2, #3, #4, #5, #6
  Set 2 - Color #2, #3, #4, #5, #6, #1
  Set 3 - Color #3, #4, #5, #6, #1, #2
  Set 4 - Color #4, #5, #6, #1, #2, #3
  Set 5 - Color #5, #6, #1, #2, #3, #4
  Set 6 - Color #6, #1, #2, #3, #4, #5

**From pressed Strip Sets, cut into 2" segments.
Keep segments together. Layout as shown below.**

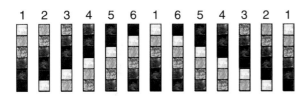

Center Row

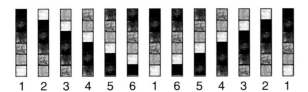

Numbers indicate Strip Set

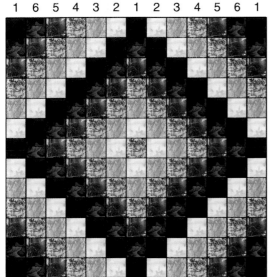

Center Strip

Finished size with borders: 27" square.

What You Will Need

- ✂ Sewing Machine with 1/4" Foot & 12/80 Needles
- ✂ YLI Wash-Away Thread
- ✂ Sulky Threads - for quilting/embellishment
- ✂ Sulky Polyester Invisible Thread
- ✂ Fabrics for "Short Trip":
  Cut 6 strips 2" x 45" light to dark
  Inner Border: 2 - 1-1/2" x 44"
  Outer Border: 3 - 4" x 44"
  Binding: 4 - 2-1/2" x 44"
  Backing: 30" x 30"
- ✂ Fabrics for Appliques:
  Fat quarter green fabric for leaves
  Scrap of yellow for flower center
  1/4 yd. of shaded fabric (light to dark) for lily.
  Scrap of blue or purple organdy for dragonfly
- ✂ Quilter's Template Plastic
- ✂ Sulky KK 2000 Temporary Spray Adhesive
- ✂ Low Loft Batting
- ✂ Iron, Pressing Surface
- ✂ Quilter's Ruler - 6" x 24"
- ✂ Rotary Cutter with sharp blade
- ✂ Cutting Mat at least 20" x 24"
- ✂ General Sewing Supplies

Applique patterns are on Pattern Sheet #2. You can make both quilt layouts from the strip sets you have cut by following the numbers which indicate the strip sets they are from. Use a 1/4" seam allowance.

Serengeti Elephant Walk
Featuring Raw Edge Applique &
Quilting with Sulky Metallic Thread

Designed and pieced by Carol Ingram –
Quilted by Evelyn Howard on a long-arm quilting machine.

Use Sulky Solvy as a quilting pattern

Fabric Credits: Sunset Fabric by Hoffman; Black Mottled Fabric designed by
Patrick Lose for Moda; Sun Fabric created with Fabric Markers on Hoffman's 200 ct. Dyer's Cloth.
Finished size: 27" x 47"

What You Will Need:

- Sewing Machine with Darning Foot
- Sulky Solvy - 8" Roll
- Sulky KK 2000™ Temporary Spray Adhesive
- Sulky Smoke Polyester Invisible Thread
- Sulky 40 wt. Rayon Thread - #1005 Black, #1181 Rust, #1055 Tawny Tan
- Sulky Original Metallic Thread - #7051 Black, #7010 Dk. Copper, #7011 Lt. Copper, #7004 Dk. Gold, #7023 Black/Silver
- Sulky 30 wt. Rayon Thread #1219 Gray
- Permanent-Ink Fabric Markers in yellow, orange and rust if you are going to shade your sun.

- Paper-backed Fusible Web
- Fabrics:
    Background fabric - 14" x 34"
    Black mottled fabric for:
      Tree, Elephants, Borders & Binding
    "Dyer's Cloth" (if you are going to "color" your own sun) or Yellow fabric for the Sun
    Zebra Striped fabric for inner and outer narrow borders
    Black backing fabric 29" x 49"
    Batting 28" x 48"
- Fine-line, permanent-ink, black marker
- Quilter's 24" Ruler, Mat & Rotary Cutter
- Iron and Pressing Surface
- General Sewing Supplies

Cut & Apply Fusible Web to Fabrics *1*

1. Cut the background fabric 14" x 34" (just below the blue color zone if using the Sunset Fabric by Hoffman).
2. From pattern sheet #1, use a fine-line, permanent ink marker to trace tree, ground elements under tree, sun and elephants to paper side of fusible web. Cut out the pieces and fuse each of them to an appropriate fabric; cut out the fabric.

Fuse Appliques to Background Fabric *2*

Since this is a raw-edge applique, fuse thoroughly, pressing first from the front, then from the back.

1. Position the sun 7-1/2" from the bottom of the background fabric and 12-1/2" from the right side edge; fuse.
2. Place the tree top 2" from the top edge of the background fabric and 2" from the right side; fuse.
3. Place the elephants in an imaginary line at the top of the darkest stripe of the fabric, 3-1/2" from the bottom, 3" from the left side, and 3" from the sun; fuse.

3 Shade the Sun

1. If you used Dyer's Cloth for the sun and/or want to add clouds over your sun fabric, use permanent-ink fabric markers in shades of yellow, orange and rust.

> *Hint: You may want to practice on a scrap of the Dyer's Cloth first before working on your fused sun. Add shading across, following the darker red lines in the background fabric.*

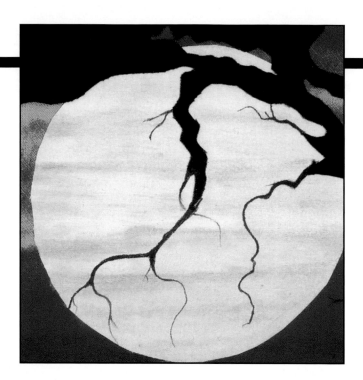

4 Add the Borders

1. Measure the sides. From the black mottled fabric, cut the borders 1" wide x length of sides. Mark center of both the wallhanging and the borders with pins. Line up centers and edges, pin and stitch. Repeat for top and bottom, dividing them into fourths with pins. Press the seams toward the darker fabric.
2. Re-measure the sides and cut the zebra fabric 1-1/2" wide x length of sides. Line up, pin and stitch.
3. Re-measure and cut black mottled fabric 4-1/2" wide x length. Line up, pin and stitch.
4. Re-measure and cut the zebra fabric 1-1/2" wide x length for the final narrow border. Line up, pin and stitch.

Layer the Quilt - Spray Baste with Sulky KK 2000

5

1. Layer the quilt by placing the backing right side down on a flat surface. Spray half of the backing with Sulky KK 2000 Temporary Spray Adhesive. Smooth the batting over the backing. Fold back the unsecured half of the batting and spray the second half of the backing. Smooth down over batting.
2. Position the wallhanging top, right side up, over the batting and backing. Fold half of the top back and spray KK 2000 onto the wrong side of the wallhanging top; smooth it down over the batting and backing. Repeat for other half. Finish securing with a few safety pins, if desired.

Add the Elephants to the Border using Sulky Solvy

6

1. **Elephant Walk Border:** Cut 2 strips of Sulky Solvy 3-1/2" wide x the length of the top and bottom borders, and 2 strips 3-1/2" wide x the length of the side borders. Using a fine-line, permanent-ink marker, trace the border elephants from pattern sheet #1 onto the Solvy. Lightly spray the borders with KK 2000 and smooth the Solvy pattern over the border, making sure that the elephants are straight, and connected at the corners. (You can reverse the direction of the elephants just by flipping the Solvy over.)
2. With Sulky 30 wt. Rayon Thread #1219 Gray in the needle and 40 wt. Rayon #1219 in the bobbin, start at the tail/trunk section and, with the feed dogs feeding or with a free-motion straight stitch (see Step #8 on page 58 if you need free-motion guidance), stitch all of the bottom half of the elephants continuously. When you reach the starting point, cross and do the upper half of all of the elephants. One start - one stop - is all that is needed.
3. To remove Solvy without submerging your wallhanging in water, wet a Q-Tip and follow the outline of the elephants to release the Solvy.

Stitch in the Ditches with Sulky Original Metallic

7

Insert a size 14/90 needle. Thread the top with Sulky Original Metallic #7010 Dk. Copper, and the bobbin with Sulky 40 wt. Rayon #1005 Black. Stitch in the ditch around all borders except, use #7023 Black/Silver in the ditch between the wide black mottled border and the outside zebra border.

Set up your machine for free-motion:
- Lower or cover the feed dogs.
- Remove the presser foot and replace it with a darning foot.
- Lower top tension slightly if needed.
- Thread the needle with Sulky Polyester Smoke Invisible Thread in the needle and Sulky 40 wt. Rayon Thread #1005 Black in the bobbin.
- Select the straight stitch, and outline stitch the fused elephants, the underside of the tree, around the bottom of the sun, and the rest of the tree trunk. This is just to add dimension and not to stitch down the raw edge.

9   Continue to Quilt

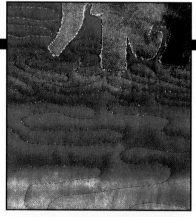
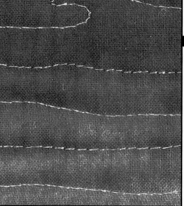
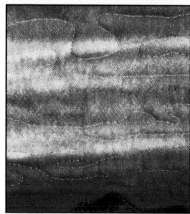
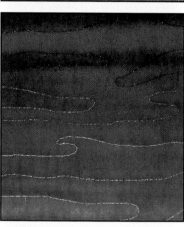

1. Thread the top with Sulky Metallic #7051 Black. Use a broad, meandering stitch from the bottom of the back-ground fabric up the entire length of the wallhanging, to the feet of the elephants, narrowing the meandering stitch as you move up towards the elephants.
2. Thread the top with Sulky Metallic #7010 Dk.Copper, and Sulky 40 wt. Rayon #1181 Rust in the bobbin. Use a narrow, meandering stitch to stitch the area surrounding the elephants, through the reddest part of the sky.
3. Thread the top with Sulky Metallic #7011 Lt. Copper. Use a narrow, meandering stitch moving upward from the top of the elephants for about 2-3".
4. Thread the top with Sulky Metallic #7004 Dark Gold, and Sulky 40 wt. Rayon #1055 Tawny Tan in the bobbin. Moving upwards, meander stitch about 2 to 3 inches of the sky area.
5. Thread the top with Sulky Metallic #7010 Dk. Copper, and Sulky 40 wt. Rayon #1181 Rust in the bobbin. Broadly meander stitch the rest of the sky to about 1" from the black border, then narrow the meander stitch to stitch the remaining inch.
6. Thread the top with Sulky Polyester Smoke Invisible Thread, and Sulky 40 wt. Rayon #1005 Black in the bobbin. Using a straight stitch, outline the top of the tree and the cut-outs in the tree.
7. Trim the wallhanging flush with outside border. Add binding and a sleeve if desired.

The Zimbabwe Elephant Walk Quilt

Sometimes as you dream of a project it can unfold before you, but othertimes it can take years to plan and execute a dream as was the case with Carol Ingram when she started this quilt 2 years ago at a Training Seminar for Sulky "Sew Exciting" Educators. Carol wanted to make this quilt as a surprise gift for her husband, Bill, as a beautiful reminder of the time they spent together in Zimbabwe, Africa.

Instructions for doing the bargello-pieced blocks can be found on page 86 of the book, **"Sulky Secrets to Successful Quilting"** 900B-13. Being the designer that Carol is, she departed from the layout in that book and created her own interpretation. Then, as she began developing the Elephant Walk Quilt and a fabric painting idea for this book (see pages 48 & 49), she decided to incorporate the Elephant Walk Panel and a painted lioness resting on a tree limb. As with her other painted quilts, she also trapuntoed the design and added further 3-dimensional leaves and free-motion

Credits: Designed, pieced and painted by Carol Ingram. Quilted with Sulky Rayon and Metallic Threads on a long-arm quilting machine by Evelyn Howard. Lioness Painting Pattern is on Pattern Sheet #4.

Fabrics: Timeless Treasures, Moda, Hoffman, Fabric Traditions and Hoffman's Dyer's Cloth.

59

Funky Chickens
Faux Hand-Turned Invisible Applique Using Sulky Solvy™

Evelyn Howard
*Director of the Annual Sulky Challenge, Designer and
Sample Maker for Sulky of Ameria*

"Some of my earliest memories of sewing are sitting under the quilting frame at the Mennonite Church and sometimes they even let me thread the needles. By chance many years later, I saw Kaye Wood's show, ordered a book and dove in. When I moved to Florida in 1997, I discovered I lived two blocks from the Sulky warehouse. This had to be serendipity. Then Joyce Drexler saw some of my samples in the fabric store where I worked, and I have been blessed to be a part of the Sulky family ever since" – Evelyn.

Finished size: 40" x 40"

Project Overview

Using the traditional Log Cabin Block, make 4 large blocks to create a background for the chickens.

First create 2 large blocks for the top, using graduated lights to darks to create a gradated sky effect. The bottom 2 large blocks will be made from graduated browns and greens, creating a "grassy ground" on which the chickens can rest. Use the Sulky Solvy-Turn Technique for each applique piece, then each piece will be appliqued down using Sulky Clear Invisible Polyester Thread and a blind hem stitch.

"I found the "Solvy-Turn Technique" so quick and easy that I will never again use the hand-turned or freezer-paper method. I get perfectly smooth edges every time!"--- Evelyn

What You Will Need:

- ✂ Sewing Machine with a blind-hem stitch
- ✂ Sulky Solvy Water Soluble Stabilizer
- ✂ Sulky KK 2000 Temporary Spray Adhesive
- ✂ Sulky Clear Polyester Invisible Thread
- ✂ Sulky 30 and 40 wt. Rayon and Metallic Threads to coordinate with chickens
- ✂ Fine-line, permanent-ink marker
- ✂ Fabrics:
  - 2 Center squares 2-1/2" x 2-1/2" each of sky blue and light green
  - Strips cut 1-1/2" x 44":
    - Blues: 15 shades numbered 1-15 light to dark.
    - Greens: 8 shades, light to dark.
    - Browns: 7 shades, light to dark.
    - Accent border: 1-1/2"
    - Border: 4"
    - Plus assorted fabrics for chickens

1 General Log Cabin

Piece using a 1/4" seam allowance

You will make 4 separate Blocks: 2 with the 15 shades of blue around blue centers and 2 with 8 shades of green and 7 shades of brown around green centers.

A

Cut a 2-1/2" center square of sky blue.

2-1/2" Center

B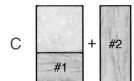

Add strip #1 (lightest blue) to the 2-1/2" blue center square. Press seam toward strip #1. Trim strip flush with center square at both ends.

C

Add strip #2 (the same color as strip #1). Press seam toward strip #2 and trim flush.

D

Add strip #3 (darker blue). Press seam toward strip #3 and trim flush.

E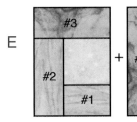

Add strip #4 (the same color as strip # 3). Press seam toward strip #4 and trim flush. **This is Round #1.** Continue adding one strip at a time in a counter-clockwise direction, pressing the seam toward the strip and trimming it flush once it is pressed out.

Make 7 rounds of 4 strips each. Two graduate darker and two graduate lighter out from the center square. Repeat to make a second blue block and 2 green/brown blocks. Trim the blocks so they are all the same size. Stitch the four blocks together. *(For color placement, see finished quilt on page 60.)*

2   Trace the Chicken Patterns

1. The patterns for the chickens are on pattern sheet #3. When you trace them with a fine-line, permanent-ink marker, use solid lines for sewing lines, slashed lines for unturned edges that will be under other pieces, and dotted lines for placement.

2. Lay Solvy over the pattern and trace each component separately. Irregular or small pieces left over from another project are perfect to use for this project as long as there is at least a 1" margin all around each pattern piece. Accurate tracing is a snap if each piece of Solvy is sprayed lightly with Sulky KK 2000 before placing it on the pattern; this will also hold the Solvy pattern onto the fabric when sewing.

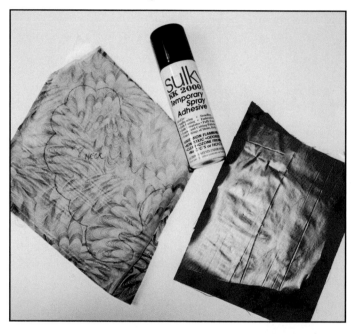

Tip:

Mark your Solvy pieces in some way so you don't accidentally reverse them. For instance, write "UP" on each piece and make sure you can read this word when you begin to cut out your pieces.

3   Create the Chicken Pieces

1. Cut apart all Solvy pattern pieces. Select your fabric for each piece and place the Solvy pattern on the right side of your selected fabric. Because you are viewing the pattern pieces as they will appear when finished, simply move and turn the Solvy pattern piece until any design feature on your fabric is within the sewing line, and going in the direction you want.

2. Straight stitch along all of the solid lines, then trim to within a scant 1/4" outside of the stitching, taking care not to trim off any portion that lays under another piece and does not need to be turned under. Turn right side out. For pieces that are sewn all the way around, carefully cut a slit in the center of the Solvy and gently turn it to the back of the applique fabric; finger press, or press with a DRY iron.

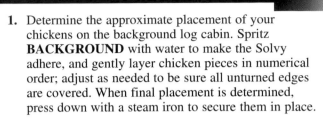

Placement of Chickens   4

1. Determine the approximate placement of your chickens on the background log cabin. Spritz **BACKGROUND** with water to make the Solvy adhere, and gently layer chicken pieces in numerical order; adjust as needed to be sure all unturned edges are covered. When final placement is determined, press down with a steam iron to secure them in place.

   DO NOT slide the iron. If a piece is loose, give it a shot of steam, then press dry.

2. With Sulky 40 wt. Rayons to match, applique stitch the chicken as desired. Evelyn used a blind hem with a relatively short stitch length. For most applique methods, no further stabilization is needed because the Solvy behind each piece is suffcient; and it will wash away without a trace leaving no stiffness or added weight.

Add Borders, Layer the Quilt, and Bind   5

Add borders, then quilt using your favorite Sulky Decorative Thread and a free-form or stencil design that best lends itself to the area being quilted.

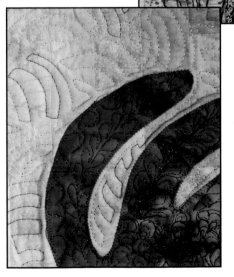

It's fun using Sulky Multi-Color Metallic Threads in different design patterns to quilt the chicken's feathers. In the green fabric areas, Evelyn used a green 30 wt. Sulky Rayon to look like grass, and a Variegated Sulky 30 wt. for the backgrounds.

Autumn Retreat
Multi-Technique Appliqued Wallhanging

Credits: Designed and quilted by Sharon Stokes on the Janome 10000 Computerized Sewing Machine. Borders embroidered by Evelyn Howard using the Amazing Designs Embroidery Card #AD3009 "Pressed Leaves Collection" by Joyce Drexler. Fabrics by Moda.

What You Will Need:

- Sewing Machine with embroidery capabilities and a large bear and fisherman design (Sharon used her Janome 10000 with the Card Reader/Writer, B hoop, Memory Card #113 and P Foot.)
- Amazing Designs Embroidery Card #AD3009 Pressed Leaves Collection by Joyce Drexler for border designs
- Sulky Tear-Easy Stabilizer
- 3 - 1 yd. packages of Sulky Super Solvy Stabilizer
- 12 - 10" x 12" pieces of black tulle
- Sulky KK 2000 Temporary Spray Adhesive
- Sulky Polyester White & Black Bobbin Thread
- Sulky 30 wt. Rayon for Fisherman Embroidery
- Sulky 40 wt. Rayon to match Satin Stitched Appliques and for Pressed Leaves Designs
- Sulky 30 wt. Cotton to piece the log cabin and for tree trunks and firewood
- Sulky 12 wt. Cotton #1005 Black for fishing line
- Sulky UltraTwist Thread - 2 - #3033 for bears, 1 - each #3038 and #3005
- Sulky Smoke Polyester Invisible Thread
- Quilter's Template Plastic
- 1 yd. of sheer to lightweight iron-on interfacing
- 1/2 yd. Steam-A-Seam 2
- Batting used: Hobbs Organic Cotton Batting with Scrim (can be quilted up to 10" apart)
- Stencil - Quilting Creations International, Inc. - MB150 - 4" Leaf
- Small fishing fly   General Sewing Supplies

FABRICS NEEDED FOR LOG CABIN
- 1/4 yd. red fabric for center square
- 1/4 yd. each of 3 different red fabrics (one can be the same as for the center squares)
- 1/4 yd. each of 5 different green fabrics
- 2 yds. light yellow fabric
- 1-3/8 yd. green fabric cut 2-1/2" wide for unpieced borders
- 1-3/4 yds. light yellow for outer border
- 3-1/3 yd. for backing
- 3/4 yd. of dark green for binding

CUTTING GUIDE FOR LOG CABIN
- Cut 16 - 2" Squares from red fabric for center squares. 16 - 2" squares from light yellow fabric for #2 square
- Cut all other strips crosswise of the fabric. This will give you approximately a 42" long strip 2" wide - do not use selvages.
- 2 - 2" strips of each red and green fabrics. (Sharon used 3 different red fabrics and 5 different green fabrics, but one red and one green will work just as well.)
- Cut 15 - 2" Strips of light yellow fabric for light side of block.

Sharon Stokes
Designer/Shop Owner
Franklin, NC

Sharon is the principal in Sharon's Quilt Shoppe, a major part of Carolina Sew & Vac Store, which is an authorized Janome and Singer Sewing Machine Dealership owned by Sharon and her husband, John. She has been teaching sewing and quilting classes since 1977. Sharon has served two years as president of the Smoky Mountain Quilt Guild and this is her third contribution to the Sulky Book Series.

Sharon won 2nd Place at the 2001 Singer Convention for her "Pineapples in my Flower Garden Quilt" that was featured in the book, **"Sulky Secrets to Successful Quilting"** 900B-13.

Sharon says, "Pumpkin, her 12 year old cat, has a 'paw' in everything she sews." She has her very own quilt next to Sharon's sewing machine.

Make a Log Cabin Quilt *1*

1. Start with a 2" red square for center block, sew #2 - 2" square (light yellow) to top of red square. Sew 2" strips clockwise in numerical sequence, being careful to position the light and dark pieces in the proper place. Place strip #3 right side down on blocks #1 and #2 (right side to right side) and sew on the right hand side starting at the top of #2 and ending at the end of block #1; fold excess of #3 back on itself with the fold even with bottom edge of #1; cut with scissors, unfold #3 strip and continue sewing the strips until your block is completed.
2. After 16 blocks are sewn, put them in proper layout using the layout guide on pattern sheet #4. Sew them together to make the top, then applique the camping scene in place. Have fun.

2 Computerized Embroidered Bears

1. Make an embroidery base sandwich: 2 layers of 10" x 12" Sulky Super Solvy, 2 layers of black tulle, then 2 more layers of Super Solvy; secure in a large embroidery hoop. Use your bear designs, embroider two sets of 2 bears; if using a Janome 10000, use the next 2 steps.
2. Insert Memory Card #113 into the Card Reader 10000 or Reader/Writer. Touch Embroidery, touch picture of the Card Reader on the screen, touch design #6. Stitch two of the bears as shown on the screen: skip steps 1 and 2 and start with step #3 by using Sulky UltraTwist #3038 for the nose and ears, #3033 for the body (step 4); #3005 for accent (step 5); and Sulky 30 wt. Rayon #1005 Black for the eyes and nose (step 6); use Sulky Black Bobbin Thread throughout.
3. Put a new base sandwich in your hoop, reverse the bear by touching Edit on the screen, then the Mirror Image; embroider two more bears.
4. After the bears have been embroidered, very carefully remove the Super Solvy by gently pulling or cutting it away from the embroidery, and trim the tulle close to the stitching with a small pair of sharp, pointed scissors.
5. Trace just the heads of the bears onto Steam-A-Seam 2; cut out and finger press onto the wrong side of each bears' head. Position the first bear on the wallhanging and use UltraTwist #3033 and a small satin stitch to stitch around the entire bear, except for the head. Repeat for the other 3 bears. Place a thick towel on an ironing board, turn the wallhanging over and place a bear on the towel, fuse the bear heads to the wallhanging with a hot, dry iron. Repeat for the other three bears. *(Do not satin stitch around the heads.)*

3 Computerized Embroidered Fisherman

1. Put a new base sandwich in your hoop and, for the Janome 10000, use Memory Card #113, Design #22; touch Edit Mode, touch Size and increase to 115%, touch okay; begin with Step 4. Using all Sulky 30 wt. Rayon: Step 4 - #1219 Gray; Step 5 - #1258 Coral Reef; Step 6 - #1035 Dk. Burgundy; Step 7 - #1179 Dk. Taupe; Steps 8 and 9 - #1128 Dk. Ecru; Step 10 - #1059 Dk. Tawny Brown; Step 11 - #1177 Avocado; Step 12 - #1005 Black.
2. After embroidery is complete, trim the Solvy and tulle as above. Fuse the fisherman in place with Steam-A-Seam 2. With the #1005 Black, free-motion a very small satin stitch around the boots. Using Sulky Smoke Invisible Thread, straight stitch along the sides of the boots and around his waist and fishing pole.
3. After the wallhanging is finished and quilted, add the fishing line by using Sulky 12 wt. Cotton #1005 Black to extend the fishing line as desired. Machine tack a very small fishing fly to the end of the line using Sulky Invisible Thread.
   Hint: It might be a good idea to cut off the tip of the hook with a small pair of wire cutters.

4 Computerized Embroidered Leaves

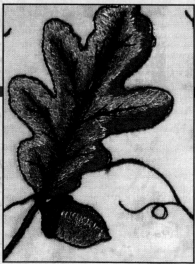

1. For Sulky Thread Color selections, follow instructions on the Amazing Designs Card #AD3009 "Pressed Leaves Collection", designed by Joyce Drexler *(see Sources - page 164)*. Put them in Editing and delete the frames and sayings. These are 4" designs but they can be enlarged up to 20% if desired.
2. Embroider them on the light yellow outer border fabric, spacing them appropriately so your borders will come out even on all sides. Using Sulky 30 wt. Cotton #1232 Classic Green, free-motion straight-stitch curls in between the leaf designs to connect the leaves together (see curl designs on Pattern Sheet #4).

Applique Designs **5**

1. See Pattern Sheet #4 for trees, tent, pond, grass, fire, canoe and paddle patterns, and drawing for proper placement. Trace designs onto Quilter's Template Plastic, label them and cut them out.
2. Cut a piece of iron-on interfacing slightly larger than the design area and iron it to the back of the selected fabrics. Using the templates, <u>turn them over</u> and trace the patterns onto the right side of the interfacing. Cut out the designs. (The interfacing prevents the edges of the applique pieces from fraying, as well as keeps the seams from the log cabin squares from showing on the applique.)
3. When appliqueing designs onto the wallhanging, use 1 or 2 layers of Sulky Tear-Easy under the stitching areas.
4. Use an applique foot (Janome P foot) and a narrow satin stitch, about 1/8" wide (a little narrower on very small objects). Lower presser foot pressure to 1 (if applicable to your machine). As you satin stitch each applique piece, use a matching color of Sulky Rayon Thread on the top and Sulky Bobbin Thread in the bobbin. Lower the top tension one or two numbers; if bobbin thread still shows on top, change to matching thread in your bobbin.
5. For the grass, use a built-in stitch on your machine and your choice of Sulky 40 wt. Rayon or Sulky 30 wt. Cotton Thread. (On the Janome 10000, Sharon used stitch #117.)

Applique Threads:

Trees, Grass around Lake, machine stitched Grass and Cattail Leaves -	**Sulky 40 wt. Rayon** #1272 Hedge Green
Lake -	#1172 Med. Weathered Blue
Tent and Canoe, light color -	#521 Nutmeg
	<u>Sulky 35 wt. UltraTwist Rayon</u>
Tent and Canoe, dark color -	#3032
Campfire -	#3043
	<u>Sulky 30 wt. Cotton</u>
Tree Trunks, Firewood, Cattails -	#1131 Cloister Brown
	<u>Sulky 12 wt. Cotton</u>
Fishing Line -	#1005 Black

Cattails **6**

1. Trace the cattails onto Sulky Super Solvy, lightly spray KK 2000 on the stitching area, and adhere the Super Solvy in place.
2. Using a narrow satin stitch and a green 40 wt. Rayon, start at the bottom of a cattail leaf and taper the width to zero by the end of each leaf. Use a brown 40 wt. Rayon and a straight stitch for the stem, then a narrow zig-zag satin stitch for about 3/8"; change to a straight stitch to finish the top of the cattails.
3. To easily remove the Super Solvy, wet a Q-tip and run it along the stitching, and the Solvy just falls away.

Borders **7**

1. Measure the center of the wallhanging lengthwise; cut 2-1/2" wide strips of green border fabric to this measurement. Using regular sewing thread or Sulky 30 wt. Cotton and a 1/4" seam, sew both side borders in place. Measure the width of the quilt across the center after the side borders are sewn. Use this measurement to cut the 2-1/2" wide top and bottom borders, and add these borders.
2. Re-measure the length through the center of the wallhanging and cut two light yellow side borders 5-1/2" wide and this long, with the embroidered leaves centered, sew in place. Re-measure the width of the wallhanging through the center after the 5-1/2" borders have been sewn onto the sides. Cut 5-1/2" wide top and bottom borders to this measurement and sew them on.

Quilt **8**

Using Sulky Invisible Thread on top and a 40 wt. Rayon in bobbin that will blend with quilt backing fabric, use a free-motion straight stitch to stitch mountains in the background of the camping scene. Stitch around all the appliques as well as the stitched leaves in the border. Stitch in the ditch of the border. Sharon also used one 4" leaf stencil (see supply list) in the unappliqued corner of each log cabin block.

Great Catch!
Applique & Quilting
with Sulky Cotton Threads

Designed by Patti Lee & Carol Ingram. Pieced by Patti Lee & Quilted by Evelyn Howard on a long arm using Sulky 12 wt. Cotton.

"Fishing"---if it were easy ... it would be called "Catching".

Now you can create this great country look with the soft, matte finish of Sulky 12 wt. and 30 wt. Cotton Thread.

Cut and piece blocks using a 1/4" seam allowance and the dimensions on the next page.

Blanket Stitch by hand or machine. Hand stitch the recipe, or "free-motion" embroider it by machine.

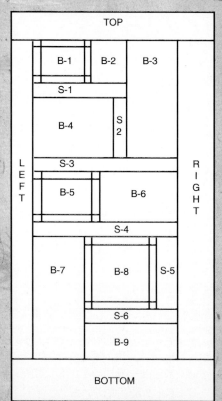

Hand-tied lures by Kenny Genawese using Sulky 12 wt. Cotton Thread.

Fabric Credits: Moda Flannels, Benartex Cottons and Hoffman Batiks.

- ✄ Sewing Machine with an open-toe applique foot, needle size 14/90
- ✄ Sulky Solvy Water Soluble Stabilizer in liquid form: 1 yd. x 20" dissolved in 8 oz. of water
- ✄ Sulky KK 2000 Temporary Spray Adhesive
- ✄ Sulky Smoke Polyester Invisible Thread
- ✄ Sulky 12 wt. and 30 wt. Cotton Threads
- ✄ Hand Needle - size 10
- ✄ Fusible Web
- ✄ Fine-line, Permanent-ink Marker or Water Soluble Marker
- ✄ Rotary Cutter, Ruler and Mat
- ✄ General Sewing Supplies

Recipe:

Stiffen the flannel by applying liquid Solvy (see ratio above) to make it easier to hand stitch the "Recipe" and "Worms" blocks; let dry. For easy tracing with a fine-line, permanent-ink marker, spray KK 2000 on the design on Pattern Sheet #2 and adhere a cut piece of Solvy to it. Trace, then spray the flannel and adhere the traced Solvy pattern for hand stitching with a backstitch using 2 strands of Sulky 12 wt. Cotton. When stitching is complete, rinse out all of the Solvy, or just remove the traced Solvy by running a wet Q-Tip gently over the stitching to release the Solvy without immersing in water.

Patti liked the stiffness provided by the liquid Solvy and let it remain in the flannel for piecing.

Option: If you have a light board, place the recipe portion of the pattern sheet over the light board, spray with KK 2000 and smooth the flannel over the pattern. Trace with a water soluble pen. Stitch, then mist with water to remove pen marks, or rinse in water.

Cotton Flies:

Around a piece of cardboard about 2" wide (business card size), wind 3 or 4 colors of Sulky 12 wt. Cotton 13-15 times. Thread a hand needle with one of the colors and slide it under and around one edge of the wound Cotton. Tie in a knot. Cut the other edge. Holding the tied end of the Cotton thread, tightly wrap another one of the 12 wt. colors around it for about 1/4". Thread a hand needle with the end of the wrapping thread and pull it under the 1/4" of wrapped thread to secure the tail. Trim to desired length. You can also wrap a small feather in with the Cotton Thread or add it with glue.

Preparing the Fabric

Fabrics:

Background: 1 yd. beige
Sashings and Borders: 1 yd. sage green
Frames and Binding: 3/4 yd. wooden look
Backing: 1-1/2 yds.
All of the appliques are done with flannel except for the fish, which are cotton. Use a 1/4" seam allowance throughout.

Cutting instructions:

Blocks: (H = heighth, W = width)

B-1 Worms:	H4-1/2" x W6-1/2"
Frame:	Two 1-1/2" x 4-1/2"
	Two 1-1/2" x 8-1/2"
B-2 Boots:	W5-1/2" x H6-1/2"
B-3 Recipe:	W7-1/2" x H16-1/2"
B-4 Campfire:	H8-1/2" x W11-1/2"
B-5 Photo:	H5-1/2" x W7-1/2"
Frame:	Two 1-1/2" x 5-1/2"
	Two 1-1/2" x 9-1/2"
B-6 Two Fish:	H7-1/2" x W11-1/2"
B-7 Three Fish:	W7-1/2" x H15-1/2"
B-8 Hat:	H6-1/2" x W8-1/2"
Frame:	Two 1-1/2" x 6-1/2"
	Two 1-1/2" x 10-1/2"
B-9 Boat:	H5-1/2" x W13-1/2"

Sashings:

S-1: 2-1/2" x 13-1/2"
S-2: 2-1/2" x 8-1/2"
S-3: 2-1/2" x 20-1/2"
S-4: 2-1/2" x 20-1/2"
S-5: 3-1/2" x 8-1/2"
S-6: 2-1/2" x 13-1/2"

Borders:

Left: 3-1/2" x 42-1/2"
Right: 5-1/2" x 42-1/2"
Bottom: 6-1/2" x 28-1/2"
Top: 4-1/2" x 28-1/2"

Sulky Cotton Threads:
12 wt.
1130 - Dark Brown
(two strands for recipe)
1271 - Evergreen
1005 - Black
1190 - Med. Burgundy
1558 - Tea Rose
1287 - French Green
1293 - Deep Nassau Blue
1181 - Rust

1184 - Orange-Red
1024 - Goldenrod
1056 - Med. Tawny Tan
1229 - Lt. Putty
1035 - Dk. Burgundy
1032 - Med. Purple
1328 - Nickel Gray
30 wt.
1180 - Med. Taupe

Fisherman's Companion Wallhanging
Appliqued with Sulky Cotton Threads

Designed and pieced by Carol Ingram. Quilted by Evelyn Howard.

Instructions for completing either of the companion Wallhangings on pages 70 & 71.

1. Trace designs from Pattern Sheet #2 onto template plastic. Cut out and label each one.
2. Cut background squares, main rectangle and framing strips. Lay out.
3. Trace around the template applique pieces onto the appropriate wool or flannel colors and cut them out. Spray the backs of all the cattail applique pieces with Sulky KK 2000 and place them as the finished wallhangings indicate.
4. Use Sulky 12 wt. Cotton to applique using a machine blanket stitch set at the longest stitch length.
5. Piece the sections together using a 1/4" seam allowance.
6. Add the leaf print sashing and border strips.
7. Use the blanket stitch to apply the rest of the appliques as shown on the finished quilts.
8. Layer the quilt, i.e., back, batting and top.
9. Spray baste the layers together using Sulky KK-2000 Temporary Spray Adhesive.
10. Quilt using Sulky 12 wt. Cotton Thread in your favorite method.
11. On the Fisherman's Quilt, add the fishing line. Carol used a 12 wt. cotton and a crochet chain stitch to create the line. A line could also be created by twisting several strands of Sulky 12 wt. Cotton together and couching them down.
12. Add the hand-made fly to the end of the lure. This one was made with Sulky 12 wt. Cotton by Kenny Genawese (see instructions on page 69).
13. Add binding. *Enjoy!*

Hunter's Companion Wallhanging
Appliqued with Sulky Cotton Threads

Designed and pieced by Carol Ingram. Quilted by Evelyn Howard.

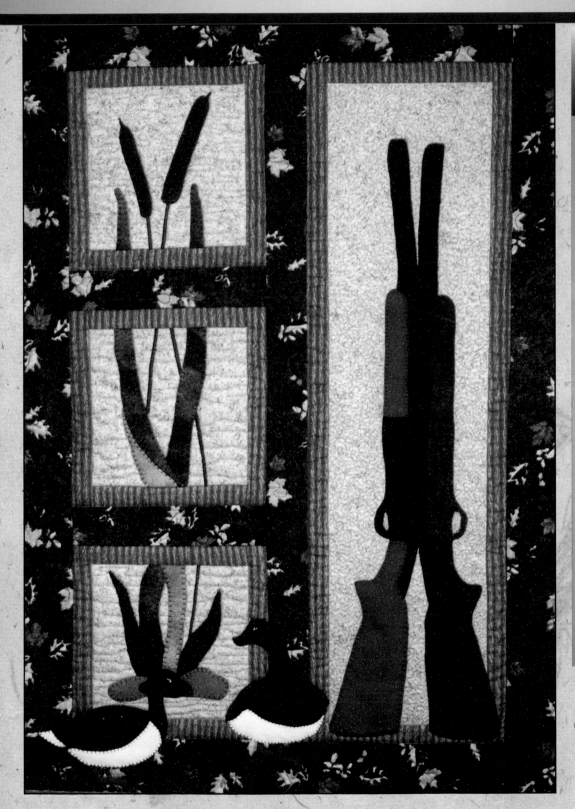

What you will need for either of the wallhangings:

✄ Sewing Machine with an open-toe applique foot, 1/4" foot, and 14/90 needle
✄ Sulky Tear-Easy Stabilizer
✄ Sulky KK 2000 Temporary Spray Adhesive
✄ Sulky Bobbin Thread
✄ Template Plastic
✄ General Sewing Supplies
✄ Moda Flannel Fabrics: 1 yd. beige cut into 3 - 8" squares for block backgrounds and 1 - 8" x 30" rectangular background
Sashings & Borders: 3/4 yd. leaf print cut Borders 3" wide Sashings 2-1/2" wide
Frames and Binding: 1 yd. wooden-look cut wooden frames 1-1/2" wide
Backing: 30" x 40"
All of the appliques are done with non-woven wool felt and 100% wool.
See Sources page 164.

✄ Sulky 12 wt. Cotton Thread for Applique:
1130 - Dark Brown
1271 - Evergreen
1240 - Smokey Gray
1058 - Tawny Brown
1149 - Deep Ecru (for Quilting)

Patterns can be found on Pattern Sheet #2

Finished size: Approx. 27" x 38"

Halloween Wallhanging
with a 3-D Applique Spider
& Sulky Solvy Spider Web

Designed, quilted, and presented by Carol Ingram
on the PBS TV Show - "America Sews with Sue Hausmann"

This Quick Halloween Wallhanging can be completed in a couple of nights or over a weekend. And it is so much fun both to shop for and to do.

Take the kids shopping with you --- they will love helping you find all the exciting fabrics and decorations.

If you want to start this project but Halloween fabrics like lace overlay web fabric are not yet available at your favorite sewing or craft shop, you can make your own with Sulky Solvy and Sulky Black Metallic Thread. . . it's easy!

Carol has drawn some really friendly ghosts to applique with Sulky Opalescent Sliver™ Metallic that simply makes them shimmer.

Don't be scared!

You can do this!

Carol Ingram and Sue Hausmann on the set of *"America Sews with Sue Hausmann"*.

What You Will Need:

- Sewing Machine with Decorative Stitches, Open-toe Applique Foot, & Narrow Braid/Cord Foot
- Sulky Super Solvy Water Soluble Stabilizer
- Sulky Black Tear-Easy Stabilizer
- Sulky Stiffy Tear-Away Stabilizer
- Sulky Black Iron-On Transfer Pen
- Sulky KK 2000™ Temporary Spray Adhesive
- Sulky 40 wt. Rayon Thread #1005 Black
- Sulky Sliver™ Metallic Thread #8040 Opalescent
- Sulky Polyester White Bobbin Thread
- Sulky Clear Polyester Invisible Thread
- Black Regular Sewing Thread
- Hot Glue Gun
- Bold-line, permanent-ink, black marker

- Quilter's 24" Ruler, Mat & Rotary Cutter
- Iron and Pressing Surface
- Optional - Teflon Pressing Sheet
- Fabrics:
  - Black Bridal Tulle - 14" x 24"
  - Halloween Border Print - 2 - 3" x 19" and 2 - 3" x 24"
  - Orange Fabric with Metallic Fleck - 14" x 24"
  - White Glittery Fabric for ghosts
  - Backing Fabric - 19" x 29"
  - Fleece - 19" x 29"
- Spider: 2 Handfuls of Fiberfill
  - Black Chenille Yarn
  - Spider "eyes"
  - Legs - Black Chenille Pipe Cleaners
  - Black Eyelash fabric for Spider Body
- General Sewing Supplies

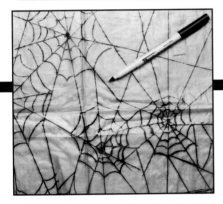

Ghosts & Web Patterns are on Pattern Sheet #1

Make the Spider Web Fabric *1*

1. Place a 14" x 24" rectangle of black bridal tulle between two layers of Sulky Super Solvy Water Soluble Stabilizer. Press with a warm, dry iron to temporarily fuse the layers together.

   *Hint: If your iron does **not** have a non-stick surface, use a Teflon pressing sheet to prevent the Solvy from sticking to the iron.*

2. With a bold, permanent-ink marker, trace the pattern of the spider webs from pattern sheet #1 onto the Super Solvy-encased netting.

   Hint: To keep the pattern and fabric from shifting while tracing, lightly spray your pattern with KK 2000 and finger smooth the Solvy-encased netting over it.

3. Thread your machine and bobbin with Sulky 40 wt. Rayon Thread #1005 Black. Select a zig-zag stitch, width 2, length 2. Attach the narrow braid/cord foot, lay the black chenille yarn in the guide on the front of the foot, and zig-zag stitch over the yarn, following all of the drawn lines. Adjust the width of the stitch if necessary to just clear the yarn. When done, soak in water to remove the Super Solvy Stabilizer. Rinse and dry.

2 Layer Web Fabric over Orange Fleck Fabric

1. Cut a 14" x 24" piece of orange metallic fleck fabric and lightly spray the right side of it with KK 2000; place the "spider web" tulle on top of it.
2. Cut 3" x 24" borders for the sides. Cut 3" x 19" borders for the top and bottom. Place each of the side borders right sides together with the orange/tulle fabric. Using a 1/4" seam allowance and regular sewing thread, stitch, keeping the edge of the fabric even with the edge of the foot. Place each of the top and bottom borders right sides together with the orange/tulle fabric, and sew. Press from the reverse side so you do not melt the tulle with the hotter setting the cotton will require.

3 Make your Ghosts

1. Using a Black Sulky Iron-On Transfer Pen, trace the ghost pattern (including faces) from pattern sheet #1 onto a piece of plain white paper.
2. Place the paper, with the traced design side down, on the right side of the white glittery fabric. Press, using a hot, dry iron to transfer the design. *Hint: By pre-heating the fabric, the transfer will be clearer and you will get more transfers from one tracing.*
3. Transfer several ghosts. Cut them out, cutting off the outside black line. Spray the ghosts with Sulky KK 2000 Temporary Spray Adhesive and place them onto your wallhanging.
4. Thread the top with Sulky Sliver Metallic #8040 Opalescent. Use Sulky White Bobbin Thread in the bobbin. Select a decorative stitch and stitch around the ghosts.

4 Layer, Stitch, Turn, Press & Quilt

1. Cut backing and fleece 19" x 29". Place the wallhanging right side down on a flat surface and spray it with KK 2000; smooth the fleece over the wallhanging. Turn it over and place the right side of the backing together with the right side of the wallhanging.
2. With regular sewing thread, stitch a 1/4" seam around all sides except, leave a 4" opening to turn. Turn. Press.
3. Quilt with Sulky Invisible in the ditch along borders.

5 Make or Add a Spider

1. Using a dinner plate as a pattern, cut a circle from black eyelash fabric. Cut a circle the same size from Sulky Black Tear-Easy Stabilizer.
2. Spray the Tear-Easy with KK 2000 and place it behind the black eyelash circle. Select a long basting stitch on your sewing machine. With regular black sewing thread in the top and the bobbin, stitch near the edge all the way around the circle. Pull up the basting thread to form an unclosed ball.
3. Place a handful of fiberfill inside. Squeeze off a portion of the circle to become the head. Tie off with black yarn.
4. Glue "eyes" in place. Twist four black chenille pipe cleaners together in the center and spread to create legs. Hot glue in place.
5. Attach to the wallhanging and watch the trick-or-treaters squeal!

Snippet® Pumpkin Patch
Applique with Sulky Sliver™ Threads

Designed, Pieced and Quilted by Carol Ingram

What You Will Need:

- Sewing Machine
- Sulky KK 2000
  Temporary Spray Adhesive
- Sulky Decorative Threads - your choice
- Fat quarter each of 4 pumpkin fabrics
  from light to dark
- Scraps of green for Leaves and Stems
- Fence and Sign Fabric
- Brown Plaid Foundation Fabric
- Twine
- Paper-backed Fusible Web
- Steam Iron and Pressing Pad
- Sharp Fabric Scissors & Template Scissors
- Template Plastic
- Fine-Line, Permanent-Ink Marker
- Chalk Marker
- General Sewing Supplies

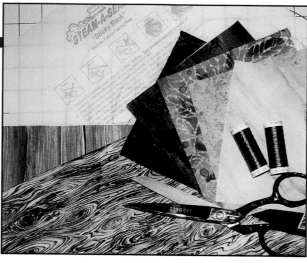

1. Gather at least 4 pumpkin fabrics ranging from light to dark to create shadows and highlights, plus fence, sign and leaf fabrics. From Pattern Sheet #1, trace posts, leaves and the sign onto paper-backed fusible web.

2. Cut out fence posts and sign. Lay the twine loosely under and over some of the posts and fuse them in place. *Hint: For easy placement of snippets for pumpkins, trace pumpkins onto template plastic. Cut out, flip over and place on the background fabric; trace around them with a chalk marker.*

3. Iron a fusible web onto the back of pumpkin fabrics, remove the release paper, cut curved snippets from them and place them, fusible side down, over the foundation fabric starting from light to dark.

4. Check that there are no gaps between fabric snippets inside the pumpkins. Once you are satisfied with the placement of the pumpkin snippets of fabric, fuse in place using a steam iron.

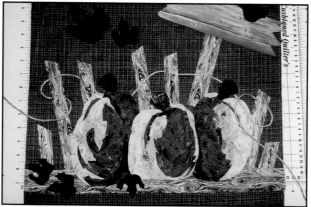

5. Add leaves and fuse them in place. Layer fleece and a backing fabric under your finished top by spraying each with Sulky KK 2000 Temporary Spray Adhesive. Quilt as desired using Sulky Threads. Square quilt. Bind.

Embroidered Overshirt & Tee
featuring Computerized, Embroidered Applique

Taken from the Designer Series Embroidery Card, "Inspirational Concepts in Sulky" #AD3000 by Joyce Drexler for Amazing Designs®

Make this easy, computer embroidered, applique duo today and wear them tomorrow.

It's easy, fast and fun!

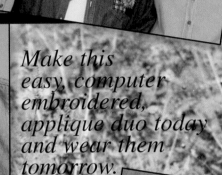

Using a fabric print for a background on which to place your embroidery, you achieve a more complicated, layered look with minimal effort. Look for fabrics like the one used here. It was actually part of a border print that was cut up and laid on point to create the interesting background. Maybe you saw Joyce wear it when she was a guest on the Fons & Porter PBS TV Show.

Joyce's "Inspirational Concepts" Embroidery Card features 20 Floral Designs with inspirational messages. You can use them as designed or just use the flowers.

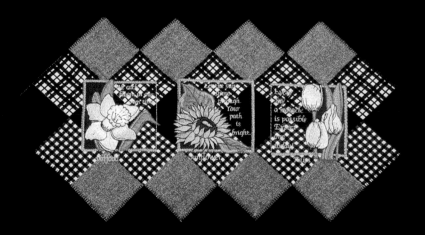

77

What You Will Need:

✂ Any Sewing Machine capable of
   Computerized Machine Embroidery
   with a hoop capable of 4" embroidery
✂ Optional: Palette™ Editing Program
✂ AD 3000 - Amazing Designs Embroidery Card
   "Inspirational Concepts in Sulky" by Joyce Drexler
✂ Sulky Totally Stable™ Iron-On Stabilizer
✂ Sulky KK 2000™ Temporary Spray Adhesive
✂ Sulky Polyester Bobbin Thread
✂ Sulky Original Metallic Thread #7023 Black/Silver
✂ 1 piece of fabric at least 12" x 20"
✂ 2 pieces of fabric 9" x 9"
✂ Steam-A-Seam 2™ Fusible Web
✂ Chalk or Air Erasable marker
✂ General Sewing Supplies
✂ Overshirt & Tee-shirt

✂ Sulky 40 wt. Rayon Thread and
   Sulky 35 wt. UltraTwist Rayon Thread

Tulip	Sun Flower	Daffodil
1. 1535	1. 1535	1. 1535
2. 3041	2. 3041	2. 3041
3. 1049	3. 1049	3. 1049
4. 3026	4. 1101	4. 3026
5. 1174	5. 1232	5. 1174
6. 1124	6. 1174	6. 1124
7. 1025	7. 3032	7. 1087
8. 1168	8. 1124	8. 1025
9. 1087	9. 3049	9. 1168
10. 1005/1024*	10. 1025	10. 1005/1024*
	11. 1005/1024*	

* Both threads through one 14/90 needle.

1 Preparation

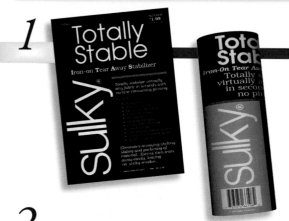

1. **Fabric:** Cut a piece at least 12" x 20", making certain that there is enough fabric surrounding the design areas to hoop securely. Prewash if desired, then press.

2. **Stabilize:** For this project, the design of the fabric dictates hooping on the bias grain. To prevent stretching, iron a piece of Sulky Totally Stable, the same size as the fabric, to the wrong side, and do not remove it until all designs have been embroidered.

2 Marking and Hooping

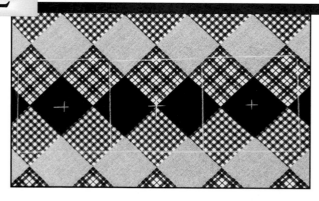 

1. **Mark placement:** Find the center point on your fabric for the finished design area and, with a chalk or air erasable marker, draw a horizontal reference line across the 20" width. Place a plus sign (+) where you want the middle design to be. To space approximately 1" between designs, mark a + 4-1/2" away on each side of the center mark (+).

2. **Hooping:** If using a small hoop for a 4" x 4" design, center the + in your hoop before you stitch each design with Sulky Thread. Rotate for desired orientation. If your machine has a large hoop 260 x 160, you will be able to sew out two designs by hooping your fabric to one end, aligning the + with the marks on the ends of the hoop. Use the layout screen to position the needle over the + for the center of the design. Embroider 2 designs and rehoop for the 3rd. With an extra large hoop, all three 4" designs may be sewn in a single hooping, but the margin will be narrower between each motif. Simply mark a horizontal line in the center of the piece and hoop

the fabric and stabilizer, aligning the marks on the fabric with the guides on the hoop. Use the layout screen to position the needle over the + for the center of the design. Sew the first design. Use the layout arrow to move to one end, rotating the design if needed. Sew the second design. Move as far as possible to the other end of the hoop and sew the third design.

3. **Take fabric out of the hoop and remove the stabilizer.** Press.

4. **Apply Steam-A-Seam 2 to the back of the embroidered fabric.** Trim to the finished shape desired.

5. **Fuse onto a tee-shirt following instructions on Steam-A-Seam package.** This project was finished with a decorative blanket stitch sewn around the applique with Sulky Rayon.

Reversible Pocket Patch using Palette 2.0

3

1. Because of the written sayings, this card is not formatted to reverse or scale. However, you can reverse just the flowers:
   • Enter the layout and editing portion of your palette program. • Click on "file"; click on "OPEN"; then browse and find AD-3000. • Open, select 24063, click on EDIT, click on SELECT ALL, click on VERTICAL MIRROR, and then click on WRITE TO CARD. You now have a mirror image of the design.

2. When sewing each flower, with the needle position over the center of the design area, advance to color zone 3 before beginning to sew, and stop on zone 10. After the flower and outline are done, follow the same steps with an edited version for mirror image.

3. Adhere to Steam-A-Seam 2 and trim to final size and shape. Fuse onto front pockets of an overshirt and finish with an applique stitch if desired.

Enjoy your new embroidered, appliqued outfit!

Autumn Sampler Wallhanging
featuring Sulky Puffy Foam™
Computer Applique

by Joyce Drexler as featured on the PBS TV Show - "America Sews with Sue Hausmann".
Features Computer Embroidery and Applique using the Signature
Series Embroidery Card, #77 AUTUMN, designed by Joyce Drexler
for Cactus Punch™. *Finished size: 21" x 21-1/2".*

Project Overview

"This is my first card in a series of Seasonal Cards for Cactus Punch as part of their Signature Series. It is packed with techniques and designs. It gives the user so many possibilites and offers designs in Applique, Embroidery, 3-D Work, Quilt Outline and Puffy Foam Work as well as many different combinations.

I know you will enjoy doing this project or pieces of it. You will want to collect all four seasons to do projects as large as a Seasonal Quilted Wallhanging or as small as a single bird on a shirt. The possibilities are endless. Try using batik or mottled fabrics for a great look."
--- Joyce

photo by Humbert Studios

Joyce Drexler and Sue Hausmann on the set of the PBS TV Show, *"America Sews with Sue Hausman"*, showing a smaller version of The Autumn Sampler Wallhanging as seen on the front cover of this book. *Fabric Credits: Benartex Fossils, Benartex International Collection and Hoffman Batiks.*

What You Will Need:

- ✂ Sewing Machine with Computer Embroidery capability
- ✂ Cactus Punch Signature Series Autumn #77, Embroidery/Applique Card suitable for machines that have a hoop that can handle a 5" x 7" embroidery or larger

- ✂ Fabrics:
  - Block's Background Fabric - Yellow/Blue Batik fabric: 1 yd.
  - Mottled Orange Sashing and Binding: 2/3 yd.
  - Green Print Borders: 1/2 yd.
  - Backing Fabric: 24" x 24"
  - Appliques - Various Scrap Fabrics
  - Frame Window - 2 mil Vinyl

- ✂ Fusible Web
- ✂ Sulky 2mm Orange Puffy Foam
- ✂ Sulky Tear-Easy, Sulky Sticky & Sulky Totally Stable Iron-On Stabilizers
- ✂ Sulky Solvy and Ultra Solvy Water Soluble Stabilizers
- ✂ Sulky KK 2000 Temporary Spray Adhesive
- ✂ Sulky Bobbin Thread
- ✂ Sulky 40 wt. Rayon Thread - see listing with Card #77
- ✂ Fairfield Low-Loft Polyester Batting
- ✂ Rotary Cutter, Mat & 24" Ruler
- ✂ Fine-line, permanent-ink markers: Red and Black
- ✂ General Sewing Supplies

- ✂ **CUTTING DIMENSIONS:**
For each section, cut Background Fabrics large enough to fit in your machine embroidery hoop. Look ahead to see what the final trim size is for each embroidered patch and cut the background fabric accordingly.

The Word Autumn Embroidered over Puffy Foam™ *1*

1. Set up the machine for computer embroidery/applique and select - *Autumn using Puffy Foam*. It is also available without Puffy Foam and as just a straight stitch outline.

2. Iron Sulky Totally Stable onto the back of the background yellow/blue batik fabric, then use KK 2000 to adhere two layers of Sulky Tear-Easy to the back of the Totally Stable. Secure all in a hoop large enough to handle a 5" x 7" embroidery. Cut a strip of Sulky 2mm Orange Puffy Foam slightly larger than the word, spray KK 2000 on the area inside the embroidery hoop where you want to stitch it, and finger press the Puffy Foam onto it.

▲Thinner 2mm   ▲Thicker 3mm

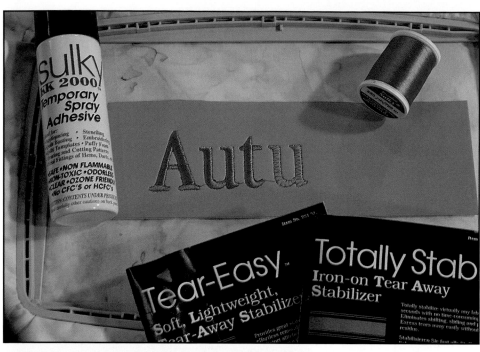

3. Thread the top with Sulky 40 wt. Rayon #1168 True Orange, and the bobbin with Sulky White Bobbin Thread.

4. Let the machine stitch out an outline that will perforate the foam and make it easier to remove when the satin stitching is completed.

5. Next, the machine will stitch out the word using a satin stitch over the Puffy Foam.

6. Remove the excess Puffy Foam by tearing it away against the stitching. (See Tip to the right.) Remove the stabilizer. Place on a towel, with embroidery side down, and press. Trim to 3-1/4" x 8-1/4". Set aside.

Tip:

You can eliminate any pokies that remain by holding a steam iron above the stitching, but not touching it, and shooting it with a blast of steam.

2 Embroider the "Pumpkins"

1. Select - *Pumpkins over Puffy or Pumpkins without Puffy.*
2. Stabilize the wrong side of the batik background fabric as you did for the "Autumn" Word on page 81. Secure fabric in a hoop large enough to handle a 5" x 7" embroidery. If you want a 3-D look, spray the design area with KK 2000 and place the 2mm Puffy Foam over it.
3. Embroider the pumpkins using Sulky 40 wt. Rayon Thread, following the color recommendations as listed on the Embroidery Card.
4. Remove excess Puffy Foam and the stabilizers. Press. Trim to 3-1/4 x 8-1/4". Set aside.

1. Select - *Cat on a Quilt with words.*
   It is also available without the words and as just a straight stitch outline.

2. Stabilize the wrong side of the batik background fabric as you did for the 2 previous embroideries. Secure fabric in a hoop large enough to handle a 5" x 7" embroidery.

3. Embroider the "Cat on a Quilt" using Sulky 40 wt. Rayon Thread, following the color recommendations as listed on the Embroidery Card.

4. Remove the stabilizers. Press. Trim to 5-1/2" x 6-1/4". Set aside.

Embroider or Applique the "Mountain Scene"

1. Select - *sig.7712 Entirely Appliqued "Spend A Day in the Woods" with saying.* It is also available as an embroidery. The Trees are also available as a separate applique or embroidery (see photos on page 16).

2. Cut the Mottled Orange Sashing Fabric large enough to fit in the hoop and to meet trimming measurement. Spray the right side with KK 2000 and smooth batik background fabric over it, right side up.

3. Stabilize the wrong side of the fabric as you did for the 3 previous embroideries. Secure in a hoop large enough to handle a 5" x 7" embroidery.

4. Use the embroidery card template to place fabric pieces. Spray the back of the fabrics with KK 2000 to temporarily hold them in place. Use the recommended Sulky 40 wt. Rayon Thread colors to Applique following Card instructions. When the first pass of stitching has completed outlining the frame of the mountain scene, stop the machine and *trim away background fabric only from around the <u>outside</u> of the satin stitched frame.* Then allow the machine to satin stitch over the cut edge.

5. Remove the stabilizer. Press. Trim to 6-1/4" x 8-1/4". Set aside.

5   Computer Applique the Fabric Leaves

1. Select - "sig. 7721 - *Six Appliqued Leaves*". They are also available as just a straight stitch outline or embroidered.
2. Secure Ultra Solvy in a hoop large enough to handle a 5" x 7" embroidery.
3. Use the template to place fabric pieces. Spray the back of the fabrics with KK 2000 to temporarily hold them in place. Use the recommended Sulky 40 wt. Rayon Thread colors to Applique following Card instructions, but do not embroider the veins and stems.
4. Remove the Ultra Solvy, let dry and put aside until you have pieced the quilt top together on page 86. Then, hoop the area where the 3-D leaves are to be placed. Spray the backs of the leaves with KK 2000. Using the template, place the leaves onto the background fabric and embroider the veins and stems.

Optional: Free-motion Applique 3-D Fall Fabric Leaves   6

This is an alternate method of making the 3-D leaves.

1. Using a fine-line, permanent-ink black marker, trace the leaves found on Pattern Sheet #2 (do not trace veins or stems at this time) onto Sulky Sticky. Cut out.
2. Using a fusible web of your choice, fuse two layers, wrong sides together, of each leaf fabric color.

Tip: Use your left-over Tear-Easy Stabilizer for a Press Cloth.

3. Use the cut-out Sticky stabilizer leaves as templates to trace around on each fabric choice.
4. Cut out the leaf groups on the traced lines.
5. Sandwich the leaves between two layers of Solvy in a German wooden embroidery hoop. Leave the feed dogs up, or set up for free-motion with the feed dogs down. Use a matching color of Sulky 40 wt. Rayon and a 3mm wide zig-zag to satin stitch along the cut edge of each leaf. Feed so that most of the zig-zag stitch is on the fabric, with just a little slightly falling off onto the Solvy.

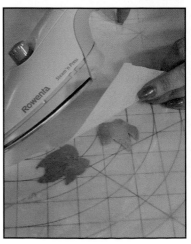

6. Remove the Solvy, let dry and put aside until you have pieced the quilt top together on page 86.

7. Then, you can make a Solvy pattern as a liftable overlay so you can see where to place the leaves correctly. Lightly spray a piece of Solvy with KK 2000 on one side only. Place the sticky side down over the leaves on the Pattern Sheet. Using fine-line, permanent-ink markers, trace the stems in red and the veins in black onto the Solvy. Remove the Solvy pattern from the pattern sheet and place the sticky side of the Solvy on the background fabric, making sure to line up the leaves properly under the viens. Smooth the Solvy down. Lift it at one end and begin placing the fabric leaves beneath it.

8. Re-smooth the Solvy over the placed leaves and use the color of Sulky 40 wt. Rayon of your choice on the top and bobbin to satin stitch the stems with a stitch width of 1; stitch the veins with a straight stitch as indicated in red in the photo to the left.

Embroider and Applique the Bird & Tree with Frame

7

1. Set up the machine for computer embroidery/applique and select - "Sig. 7705, *Chickadee in tree in Window Frame - All Embroidered with Frame Appliqued*". It is also available without the Frame and as just a bird (Chickadee) with embroidered leaves or appliqued leaves. The frame can also be embroidered separately and a photo transfer or landscape print could be used instead of the Chickadee in the Tree.

2. Cut batik background fabric large enough to fit in the hoop and to meet the trimming measurement.

3. Stabilize the wrong side of the fabric as you did for the other appliques. Secure in a hoop large enough to handle a 5" x 7" embroidery.

4. Use the recommended Sulky 40 wt. colors to embroider the Tree and Bird following the Card instructions; stop at #8.

5. Choose *sig. 7704, Embroidered Window Frame* --- add 2 mil vinyl to represent the window pane, if desired, following instructions on the embroidery card.

6. Remove the stabilizers. Press. Trim to 7" x 8-3/4". Set aside.

85

1. **The Embroidered Patches should be trimmed as follows:**
   - Autumn Word - 3-1/4" x 8-1/4"
   - Pumpkins (Puffy Applique) - 3-1/4" x 8-1/4"
   - Cat on Quilt (Embroidered) - 5-1/2" x 6-1/4"
   - Bird, Tree in Window Frame 6-3/4" x 8-3/4"
   - Mountain Scene - 6-1/4" x 8-1/4"
   - Fall Leaves Patch --- cut a piece of Batik background fabric 2-3/4" x 7".

2. **Sew the Patches together into Units by adding the Mottled Orange Sashing Strips:**
   Sew by laying right sides together and using a 1/4" seam allowance throughout. Press as you go. (Refer to finished Wallhanging on page 80 and layout on Pattern Sheet #2.) Sew the Left Unit by combining the "Mountain Scene" with the "Cat on a Quilt" using a 1-1/2" x 6-1/4" Sashing Strip between them. To sew the Right Unit, add to the Fall Leaves Patch a 1-1/4" x 2-3/4" Sashing Strip to the top and a 1-1/2" x 2-3/4" strip to the bottom. Sew the "Bird, Tree in Window Frame" and the "Fall Leaves" together. Add a 1-1/4" x 3-1/4" Sashing Strip to the left side of the Pumpkin Patch. Sew this to the previously combined "Bird, Tree in Window Frame" and the "Fall Leaves". Sew Unit 1 to Unit 2. Next, sew a 1-1/4" x 14-1/4" Sashing Strip to both sides. Complete the Sashing by sewing a 1-1/4" x 16-1/2" strip to the top and bottom. Press. Square up.

3. **Outer Borders:** Measure down the center of the sashed wallhanging and cut outer borders 3-1/2" x that measurement. Pin one border to each of the left and right sides of the wallhanging, right sides to right sides, and sew them together. Measure across the center and cut top and bottom borders. Sew to wallhanging. Press.

4. **Layer, Baste with KK 2000, and Quilt:**
   With right side down, lay out the backing fabric that is cut 2" larger all around than the wallhanging. Spray the wrong side with KK 2000. Smooth Low-Loft Batting or Fleece (cut the same size as backing) over the backing fabric. Spray the wrong side of the wallhanging with KK 2000 and center over batting. Smooth.

5. **Quilt and Finish:** Quilt in the ditch with Sulky Clear Invisible Thread using a straight stitch. Quilt Borders with Sulky 30 wt. Rayon #2247 using a stipple stitch, or use the Leaf Stipple pattern on Pattern Sheet #2. Trim and square up the quilt.

6. **Binding:** Cut binding 1-1/2" wide. To make continuous binding, put wrong sides together at short ends of each strip and sew one to another. Then, fold wrong sides together lengthwise. With right sides together, match the raw edges of the binding to the raw edges of the wallhanging. Pin in place. Sew together. Fold binding to the back of the quilt and Hand Whip Stitch it in place. **Add a label** to the back if desired. Hand Whip Stitch it in place.

Nature through the Seasons
Featuring Traditional Satin Stitch & Blanket Stitch Applique

"I love using Sulky 30 wt. and 40 wt. Rayon Threads on my designs. The quality of these threads help add a beautiful sheen to my products. Sulky also has an extraordinary array of colors which allows me to monochromatically outline and accessorize my designs. Sulky KK 2000 Temporary Spray Adhesive is a must for all appliquers and quilters. It gives me the temporary hold that I need when I play around wtih fabrics and colors. I like using KK 2000 when I place large pieces of fabric that I then applique or hand stitch around." --- Patti

Patti O'Malley
*Designer and Owner
of Mulberry Tree Designs*

Patti has been sewing and creating designs for years ... about 18. This was the same time she started her first teaching job. Patti has always had a passion for the arts. In 1995, as her life was overly abundant with shirt orders, her children's schedules and activities, and teaching, she decided to start a pattern company. Currently there are 64 patterns in the line. She has been using Sulky Threads and products for the past several years. Patti continues to design innovatively and looks forward to having her company grow while she teaches part-time.

1 Fuse Background Squares

1. Apply a paper-backed, fusible web to the natural colored fabric and cut out 4 - 6" x 7" pieces for the background.

2. Cut 1 of each of the 4 different seasonal background scene fabrics 4" wide by 4-1/4" high. Use Sulky KK 2000 Temporary Spray Adhesive to adhere these smaller patches to the natural background fabric, placing them 1" from the top, 1-1/2" from the bottom, and 1" in from each side.

2 Make the Flower Box

1. Use a pencil to trace the patterns from Pattern Sheet #2 for the Summer Path, the window, window grids, and window box shapes onto the paper side of fusible web.
2. Cut out, place and fuse the fabrics using these pictures as a guide.
3. Create the flowers and greenery with a small stencil brush by blotting the paint (or use permanent fabric markers) onto the window box area. Patti used green, cranberrry and purple.

3 Other Seasons

1. Trace the patterns (from Pattern Sheet #2) onto the fusible web and apply them to the assorted fabrics chosen for your design elements.
2. Cut out, place and fuse the fabrics following the photos on page 89 as a guide.
3. Trace the season names that are written in reverse and follow the Sulky Iron-on Transfer Pen instructions on the package to transfer them to your base fabric, then go over them with a permanent ink marker; or use a wide-line, permanent-ink marker and the season names that are not reversed, as a guide to draw them free-hand onto your base fabric.

What you will need:

- ✂ Sewing Machine
- ✂ Sulky KK 2000 Temporary Spray Adhesive
- ✂ Sulky Decorative Rayon Threads - your choice of colors in 30 or 40 wt.
- ✂ Lightweight fusible web with a paper-backed release sheet
- ✂ Fabrics:
  1/4 yd. natural colored fabric for bases
  4 - 4" x 4-1/2" pieces assorted colors for seasonal backgrounds
  Scraps for seasonal applique elements
- ✂ Regular lead pencil
- ✂ Sewing thread
- ✂ Stencil brush
- ✂ Paints: Delta Creamcoat Acrylic Paints or Folkart Acrylic Paints *(or permanent fabric markers could be used)*
- ✂ Americana DecoArt Fabric Painting Medium DAS10
- ✂ Black or Brown Sulky Iron-On Transfer Pen or a wide-line, permanent-ink marker
- ✂ General Sewing Supplies

Tip:

Summer

Heat the fabric first for a better, darker transfer. Remember, this is a permanent transfer pen.

Shake the pen before using.

On the top of your machine, use Sulky 40 wt. Rayon Threads that coordinate with your fabric choices. As appropriate, use either black or white Sulky Bobbin Thread in your bobbin. Use a 2 to 3mm wide satin stitch throughout.

1. **Window box:**
   Use a brown thread to satin stitch around the window box, then the brown branches on the Spring, Summer and Fall scenes. Choose a light green thread to satin stitch the light green leaves on the Summer scene.

2. **Spring birdhouse, windows:**
   Satin stitch around the birdhouse. Choose a thread for the nests. When satin stitching around the nests, move your fabric around to give the stitching a "jerky, twiggy" look. Using a blanket stitch or other decorative stitch, stitch around the windows and the grids.

3. **Winter twigs and dark green boughs and leaves:**
   Satin stitch the winter twigs. Using a dark green thread, stitch the boughs on the Winter scene and the leaves on the Fall and Spring scenes. Patti used a small zig-zag stitch on the Spring leaves. With a dark brown thread, satin stitch a line up the green boughs on the Winter scene.

4. **Green grass, eggs, pussy willows, pumpkins and bird-buttons:**
   To stitch the grass around the Spring birdhouse, use a dark green thread first, then a light green thread to do a satin stitch with a fast, sideways, jerky movement. Satin stitch around the eggs. Using the same stitch you used for the Spring leaves, stitch around the pussy willows. Use an orange Sulky Rayon to satin stitch around the pumpkins. Sew on the 4 bird buttons.

   These bird buttons are available through Mulberry Tree - see below

5. **Outside leaves, curly-Q's and ditty dots:**
   Fuse down the leaves at the corners of each patch. Applique around them using both a light and a dark green thread. Use a bold, permanent-ink marker to draw on the curly-Q lines. Be sure to sign your masterpiece.

Look for Mulberry Tree patterns at your local fabric store.

To contact Mulberry Tree:
Phone: 253-862-5353
Fax: 253-862-5356
Web site: www.mulberrytree.net
E-mail: mulbtree@worldnet.att.net

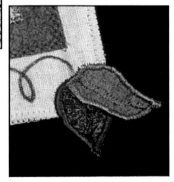

Daisy May
Window Applique
Cameo Vest from a Print

Presented by Joyce Drexler on the PBS TV Show -
Martha's Sewing Room

Fabric Credits:
Panel print
by Springs Industries.
Upholstery fabric
over-dyed by
Evelyn Howard.

◀ Back view of vest.

90

"Designer's Choice" Vest Pattern
by Lorraine Torrence Designs
2112 S Spokane St., Seattle, WA 98144
1-800-369-4974
lorrainebow@sprynet.com

What You Will Need:

- ✀ Sewing Machine with Computerized Embroidery Capability
- ✀ Amazing Designs Embroidery Card #AD3000 "Inspirational Concepts in Sulky" by Joyce Drexler
- ✀ Sulky Threads for Embellishing
- ✀ Sulky Solvy Water Soluble Stabilizer
- ✀ Liquid Solvy
- ✀ Sulky Totally Stable Iron-on Stabilizer
- ✀ Sulky Tear-Easy Stabilizer
- ✀ Sulky Soft 'n Sheer Cut-Away Stabilizer
- ✀ Sulky KK 2000 Temporary Spray Adhesive
- ✀ Sulky Smoke Polyester Invisible Thread
- ✀ White Washable Marker
- ✀ Stencil Cutting or Wood Burning Tool
- ✀ Cat panel or feature fabric of your choice
- ✀ Vest Pattern with Fashion Fabric as required for Vest of your choice
- ✀ Extra fabric for window liner, approx. 13" x 16"
- ✀ Fine-line, permanent-ink marker
- ✀ General Sewing Supplies

Preparing the Fabric

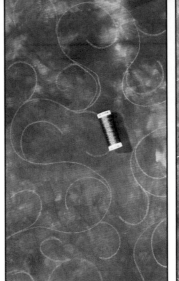

1. Cut out vest pattern pieces. Set aside all but the two fronts. If embellishing both fronts, apply liquid Solvy to both, otherwise, only apply to left front. Dry and press. Draw gentle curves and 1/2 circles with a White Washable Marker.

2. Using Sulky 30 wt. Rayon Variegated Thread #2131 Vari-Khakis, free-motion straight stitch the curves and half-circles.

   Note: Evelyn over-dyed this yellow upholstery fabric with green to give it a mottled, hand-dyed look.

Select Motif Design Area for Cameo Window, and Embellish

1. Lay a piece of Solvy over left vest front and use a fine-line, permanent-ink marker to trace vest shape onto it. To preview selection, trace the window shape from pattern sheet #2 onto the largest area of the vest shape and lay it over the motif area you have selected from the feature fabric. Trace the outline of the major features surrounding your selected motif onto the Solvy pattern. Cut out motif from the feature fabric, leaving a generous margin on all sides. Put aside the Solvy window pattern.

2. Iron Sulky Totally Stable onto the back of the cut-out motif. Free-motion embellish as desired. Evelyn highlighted the cat with Sulky 40 wt. Rayon #1056 Med. Tawny Tan and #1001 Bright White; the birdhouse with UltraTwist #3019 and #3032; and the leaves with Sulky 40 wt. #1208 Mallard Green.

91

3 Make the Cameo Window

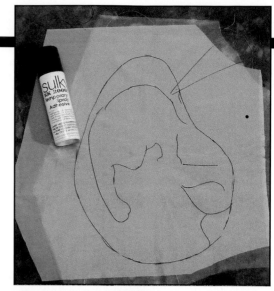

1. Cut a piece of any cotton fabric for the window lining at least 2" larger all around than the window. Place the left vest front right side up and spray with Sulky KK 2000 on the area where the window will be placed. Place the window lining fabric wrong side up on the vest front. Spray KK 2000 on the whole left vest front fabric (including the window lining) and place the Solvy pattern on top, using the markings traced from the feature fabric to place correctly.

2. Using regular sewing thread, straight stitch on the drawn window line. Cut away both layers of fabric inside the window line, leaving approximately a 1/2" seam allowance. Clip all the way around. Do not remove the Solvy that remains.

3. Turn through to the back. Trim Solvy and lining, leaving a 1" seam allowance; press. Spritz the 1" seam allowance with water. Re-press to bond the pieces for a sharp, stable edge.

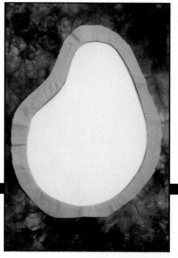

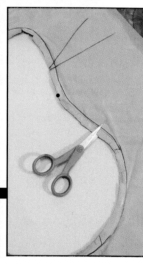

4 Insert Embellished Print

1. Position embellished motif behind the window, using the Solvy pattern as your guide for placement; pin in place.

2. With a matching Sulky 30 wt. solid color or blending 30 wt. variegated, topstitch from the right side about 1/8" from the edge, using an edge foot, if available.

5 Add Leaves from the Print

1. If your feature fabric has leaves, cut, place and fuse them (see the photo as a placement guide) using your favorite fusible web.

2. Using Sulky Smoke Polyester Invisible Thread, select an applique stitch to stitch down the edges of the leaves.

3. Wash out Solvy. Dry and press.

Optional - Right Front of Vest

6

1. Because Evelyn's fabric had flowers and leaves on the right vest front, she free-motion straight stitched several times over the leaf outline using Sulky 40 wt. Rayon #1208 Mallard Green.

2. She outlined the flowers several times using the free-motion straight stitch and Sulky 30 wt. Rayon #1080 Orchid and #1032 Med. Purple.

3. She detailed and shaded the flower centers using a scribbling straight stitch and Sulky 30 wt. Rayon #1156 Lt. Army Green.

Embroider Flower Appliques

7

1. Hoop 3 layers of white or black Sulky Soft 'n Sheer Stabilizer.

2. On the Soft 'n Sheer, embroider the daisies and leaves from the Amazing Designs Embroidery Card AD3000 after advancing past the first two zones. Stop the stitching when it starts lettering. Evelyn sewed two sets of daisies with Sulky 40 wt. #1001 Bright White and one set with #1080 Orchid. The centers are #1159 Temple Gold.

3. Remove from hoop and cut away the Soft 'n Sheer close to the edge of the design.

4. Melt away remaining Soft 'n Sheer with a stencil cutting or wood burning tool.

5. Repeat the previous 4 steps to make as many flowers as you want to place on the vest.

Add Computer Embroidered Flowers

8

1. Spray KK 2000 on the back of each flower applique and place in your desired arrangement on the right vest front; securely fasten them using Sulky Clear Polyester Invisible Thread to stitch around the edges with either a straight stitch or a narrow zig-zag.

2. Construct the vest following vest pattern instructions.

Tip:

If Joyce wants to see how colors work in a computerized embroider design, or to do a test sew-out, she does it on Soft 'n Sheer and then saves them for a project such as this one.

Tuxedo Vest
Applique the Sulky
KK 2000 Way!
No Fusible Web - No Pins!
Designed by Carol Ingram and
presented on the PBS TV Show - "America
Sews with Sue Hausmann"

**Combine
Photo Transfer
Appliques,
Fabric Pieces,
Computer
Embroidered
Designs &
Machine
Stitches!**

Now,
you can
get Carol's
Snow Folks on fabric
in three different ways
as well as on a computer
embroidery card.
**Look for them at your
favorite sewing or fabric store,
or, if you cannot find them,
you can order on-line from
www.speedstitch.com.
They are as cute as a button!**

*Using KK 2000 to secure your applique, you can make an eye-catching
Designer project with sparkling Sulky Red Sliver™ or Holoshimmer™
Metallic and your decorative machine stitches.*

*The vest is appliqued both with a pre-embroidered Snowman from
Carol's "Snow Family" Embroidery Card along with a sample of her
original color art work transferred to Viking's Colorfast Printer Fabric.*

94

What You Will Need:

- Sewing Machine with Embroidery Unit
- Open-Toe Applique Foot, Edge Stitch Foot or 1/4" Foot
- Metallic Needles Size 14/90
- 2 one yard packages of Sulky Black Totally Stable Iron-On Stabilizer
  Optional: Sulky Black Soft 'n Sheer Stabilizer to use between vest layers for added stability
- Sulky KK 2000™ Temporary Spray Adhesive
- 2 spools Sulky Sliver Metallic #8014 Red
- Sulky Poly Deco #1005 Black for Bobbin
- 1 or More Embroidered Snowmen from Cactus Punch Signature Card #22 by Carol Ingram
- Wood Burning Tool

- 2 Snowmen designs transferred onto Viking's Colorfast Printer Fabric Sheets, or use cut-outs from Carol's new Snow Follies by Fabric Traditions
- Fabrics:
  1 yd. Dark Red Fossil Fern by Benartex
  1/8 yd. Green Fossil Fern for Trees
  1/2 yd. 60" Black Lightweight Wool or Poly-Blend Suiting
  3/4 yd. Black Lining Material
- Favorite Tuxedo Vest Pattern
- 3 buttons
- Fine-Line, Permanent-Ink Black Marker
- Black Construction Thread
- Black Velcro Strips - 1/2" wide
- General Sewing Supplies

Cut, Stabilize & Spray KK 2000   *1*

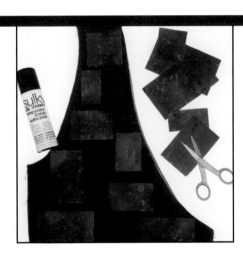

1. Cut 1 set of vest pattern pieces from the black suiting fabric or lightweight wool and one set from the black lining fabric. Set lining pieces aside for now.

2. Iron Sulky Black Totally Stable onto the wrong side of the right and left vest pieces.

3. From the red Fossil Fern Fabric, cut out 16 to 20 squares and rectangles, at least 2-1/2" x 2-1/2" and no larger than 4" x 4"; spray Sulky KK 2000 Temporary Spray Adhesive on the wrong side of them and position them in a pleasing manner on both of the vest fronts. No pinning !!!!

Stitch Around Red Fabric Pieces   *2*

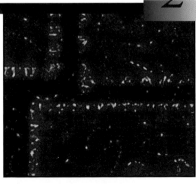

1. Using Sulky Poly Deco #1005 Black in the bobbin, thread the top with Sulky Sliver Metallic #8014 Red.
2. Using various decorative stitches of your choice, applique each red fabric piece onto the vest fronts.
3. Add optional fabric applique, green trees - pattern above.

3 Position & Applique Snowmen - Prints/Photo Transfers/Embroideries

1. Spray Sulky KK 2000 on the wrong side of the Snowmen designs that you have transferred onto Viking's Colorfast Printer Fabric Sheets. *(DO NOT SPRAY THE VEST.)* You could also use cut-outs of Carol's Fabric Snowmen. Position as desired on the left vest front and applique using a decorative stitch such as the blanket stitch, and Sulky Sliver Metallic #8014 Red.

2. Embroider the snowmen on Sulky Soft 'n Sheer White Stabilizer, following the instructions for your computerized embroidery machine. Cut away the excess stabilizer leaving about 1/8". Use a wood burning tool to burn away the remaining Soft 'n Sheer.

3. Spray the back of the embroidered snowmen with KK 2000 and position them as desired on the right vest front. Applique using a medium zig-zag stitch and Sulky Sliver Metallic #8014 Red.

4 Lining the Vest

1. Remove the excess stabilizer from the back of the vest pieces.
   Optional: An inside layer of Sulky Black Soft 'n Sheer Stabilizer may be added for additional stability while quilting the final stitched piece, and to provide more body since this vest may be worn under a jacket or over a blouse or dress as a wardrobe accessory.

2. Spray the wrong sides of the lining pieces with KK 2000 and adhere them to the wrong sides of the appliqued vest right and left fronts. *No pinning!!*

5 Quilt the Vest

1. Using Sulky Sliver Metallic #8014 Red, free-motion stipple stitch over both vest fronts, stitching over some of the squares and avoiding others for a decorative, textured look.

2. After stippling, trim any irregular vest edges before applying the binding.

3. From the vest fabric, cut a 2-1/2" wide strip on the bias as long as is needed to go around the vest edges. Fold in half lengthwise and press. Match the raw edges of the bias binding to the raw edges of the right side of each of the vest fronts and use regular sewing thread to stitch on the right side of the garment with a 1/4" seam allowance. Fold over the bias binding toward the back of the vest and stitch the folded edge down by hand or machine. Leave two 3" to 6" extensions (depending on your waist measurement) at the back edges for the back belt.

4. Overlap the right vest front over the left vest front (approximately 1/2") at the center and stitch them together.

5. Add three buttons. Apply a 1" Velcro closure at the neck edge and a 2" Velcro closure on the waist ties.
   Optional: Extended waist strips may be left long and tied at the back waist without adding the Velcro closure.

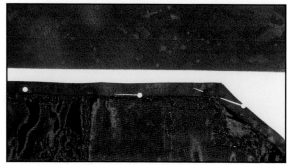

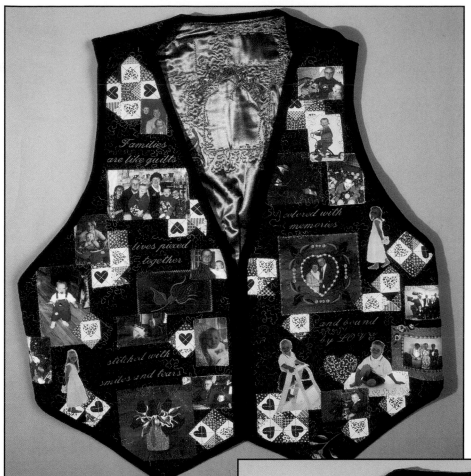

The Family Vest

The Family Vest was first created by Husqvarna Viking Educator Bonnie Colonna, who is based in Colorado Springs, Colorado. For several years, Bonnie has been creating with fabric pictures, using the transfer process on art from the Internet and photos. When Sue Hausmann sent her a package of Husqvarna Viking Colorfast Printer Fabric Sheets, she was so excited about being able to print the fabric with her ink jet printer, and that the fabric picture is soft, can be ironed, and is colorfast, that she created a special vest for Sue to wear on her PBS-TV show, "America Sews with Sue Hausmann".

Sue wore it on the Sulky program with Joyce Drexler and Joyce liked it so much that she asked to include it in this book. One of Bonnie's special techniques is to line the fabric on which she builds the collage of pictures and embroideries with a "sunback" (flannel backed) lining fabric that is usually used to line outerwear coats. The flannel layer of the lining fabric eliminates the need for batting, making the finished vest more comfortable and more flattering to wear.

The basic pattern with open side seams that close with buttons and buttonholes makes the vest easy to fit.

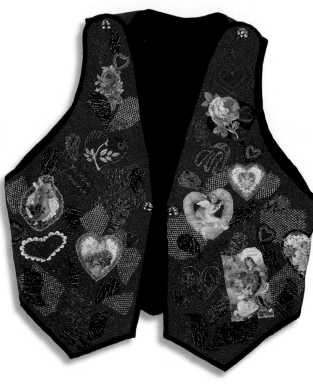

Other great examples of Photo Transfer Fabric vests that were made by Bonnie Colonna, Viking Freelance Education Consultant.

She used nostalgic holiday wrapping papers and cards for images.

A Herky-Jerky™ Sweatshirt
A Unique Applique Stitch Technique using Sulky 30 wt. Cotton Thread

Kathleen Parman
Owner of Bright Ideas Design Co.

Kathleen started her pattern design business in 1997 with an emphasis on sport quilts for sport enthusiasts. In 2000, Kathleen's newest Herky-Jerky stitched designs, all inspired from bible verses, were introduced and became an instant hit with the quilting crowd. Kathleen designs from her home in Wausau, WI, where she also keeps track of her husband and two growing boys. In her spare time, Kathleen is a part-time organist for her church, volunteers within the Boy Scout organization, and supports her family's active sports commitments. Kathleen attended the University of Wisconsin - Whitewater, and obtained a degree in Business Administration with an emphasis on accounting. She used her skills for 12 years, working for two large corporations as an accounting manager, and then was let go. Although it seemed devastating at the time, Kathleen was blessed with the inspiration and creativity to start up Bright Ideas Design Co. and she hasn't looked back since.

*Look for Kathleen's Herky-Jerky patterns at fine sewing stores in the USA and Canada.
If you cannot locate her patterns, contact Bright Ideas, 4010 Pine Tree Rd., Wausau, WI 54403-2246*

- ✂ Sewing Machine
- ✂ Sulky Tear-Easy Stabilizer
  (or, use Sulky Soft 'n Sheer if using T-shirts or lightweight fabrics)
- ✂ Sulky KK 2000 Temporary Spray Adhesive
- ✂ Sulky 12 wt. Cotton Thread #1005 Black for stitching down the neckline and shirt bottom by hand
- ✂ Sulky 30 wt. Cotton Thread #1005 Black for the Herky-Jerky stitching
- ✂ Zip-Lock Bags
- ✂ Fine-line, Permanent-ink Marker
- ✂ General Sewing Supplies

- ✂ Sulky Black Polyester Bobbin Thread
- ✂ 1/4 yd. Heat 'n Bond Light Fusible Web
- ✂ Fabrics:

Selecting Fabrics: The black fabric is solid, not mottled. All other fabrics are either mottled, marbled or batik to give a "sun shining through a window" effect for the pieces. Certainly this flower can also be made up using floral fabrics.

- 1/4 yd. black fabric for 3 background blocks
- 9" square pieces for each sky blue, green stem, and golden-yellow petals
- Scrap of rust/brown for flower centers

*"Herky-Jerky wearable art and quilt projects require several Sulky products in order for the quilter to be successful. Sulky provides me with the options of numerous stabilizers to meet my needs. I use Tear-Easy Stabilizer behind all of my design blocks for wall quilts, Sulky Cut-Away Soft 'n Sheer Stabilizer inside my t-shirt work, and I also love Sulky Solvy Stabilizer for tea towels where I prefer no visible stabilizer to remain after I'm finished stitching. The other important Sulky products I use are **Sulky's new 12 wt. and 30 wt. Cotton Thread** and Sulky KK 2000 Temporary Spray Adhesive. Cotton thread is a must for my stained glass blocks and nothing works quicker than a squirt of KK 2000 to hold the blocks to my sweatshirt for stitching."--- Kathleen*

1 Trace the Designs & Prepare the Applique

Base: Fusing and stitching "stained glass" pieces to a solid background rectangle creates each block. To create the base black rectangles that your pieces will be fused to, cut three rectangles, 4" x 5-3/4". Set aside.

Trace: From the design pattern on pattern sheet #3, use a fine-line, permanent-ink marker to trace all of the shapes three times onto the paper side of Heat 'n Bond Light (the designs are printed in reverse of what your block will be). You do not need to trace the outline rectangle. Number each petal which will help when placing them onto your black rectangle fabric. Kathleen likes to trace all of the shapes for one flower block as they appear and then cut the fusible web apart into the individual pieces. Remember, we are only separating the shapes, not cutting on the actual tracing lines yet.

Cut: Working one flower block at a time, iron the fusible web pieces onto your appropriate fabrics. (Stem fused to green fabric, petals fused to yellow, etc.) Have plastic bags ready to keep each block's pieces together, then cut out the pieces, cutting on the actual tracing line.

Fuse: Working one block at a time, remove the fusible web paper backing from one block's pieces and reassemble, realigning the pieces of the flower block onto one of your black rectangles. To help position the little pieces, use the design pattern, your numbering on each piece, and the photograph. Remember this design pattern is now a reverse image of what you are laying down (petal #3 should be in the 9:00 o'clock position now). **NOTE: Allow approximately 1/4" as a framing border around your pieces. Take your time arranging the pieces. Your pieces won't always be in the exact same spot on each flower block, and that's okay. Actual stained glass isn't exact either. Iron the pieces in place once you have them positioned.**

Hint: Kathleen found that ironing the lower sky and stem pieces first and then making a second pass at positioning all of the petal pieces made life easier than trying to control all of the little pieces at one time. Repeat this process for the remaining two flower blocks.

Position the Blocks on the Shirt or Sweatshirt 2

Work with one block at a time to position them onto your sweatshirt. Beginning with the center block, spray the back of it with Sulky KK 2000 Temporary Spray Adhesive and place it where desired. Then spray the remaining two blocks with KK 2000 and place them to the left and right of the center block.

Stabilize the back of the Shirt or Sweatshirt 3

Kathleen suggests that you use Sulky Soft 'n Sheer under a T-Shirt or other lightweight fabric like quilt squares. She recommends using two layers that are at least 2" larger all around than the stitching area. **Adhere the layers together and keep them in place by spraying KK 2000 on the stabilizer, *not the shirt.***

Set up your machine for Free-Motion Stitching 4

1. Lower or cover the feed dogs (check your machine instruction book for setting up for darning).
2. Replace the regular presser foot with a darning foot.
3. Thread a new 14/90 needle with Sulky 30 wt. Cotton #1005 Black or try Sulky 12 wt. Cotton which is thicker. Bobbin should also contain the same 30 wt. Cotton or Sulky Black Bobbin Thread.
4. Select the straight stitch setting.

Sulky 12 wt. Cotton

Sulky 30 wt. Cotton

You really should practice this stitch prior to stitching your first flower block. Practice makes closer to perfect! You may find that securing the stitching area in a German hardwood embroidery hoop will give you the best control, and less stress on your arms and neck; the stitching, however, can be easily accomplished without a hoop by simply holding the shirt with both hands and keeping it flat against the throat plate of the machine while stitching. The "star-like" stitching to the right is an example of what your Herky-Jerky stitching can look like! We are wiggling our machine stitching over and around our fused applique pieces. This is a most foolish (but beautifully effective) machine applique stitch. *It's the easiet applique stitch yet!*

5 Apply the Herky-Jerky Stitching

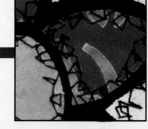

Place your first block under the presser foot and manually lower your needle through the fabric and back up along an edge of one of the fused pieces. Stop. Using your upper thread, pull the bobbin thread up through the fabric so that you have both threads in your left hand. Hold them to secure your first stitches, then clip these threads away. (Holding onto them longer will be distracting and can affect the quality of your stitching.) Take off in a Herky-Jerky, PETITE circular, triangular motion while running your machine with a relatively steady stitching rhythm as you move the block around to stitch along the piece edges. Stitch on the fused pieces and off of them into the background fabric. Follow around all of the fused pieces on your flower block. Maneuver around all of the pieces and "hop" across the background fabric to each of the pieces without stopping to cut threads and restart. Finish up your stitching by Herky-Jerky stitching the black rectangle outer edges to the sweatshirt, stitching on the black rectangle and off onto the sweatshirt. Repeat for other blocks.

6 Finishing your Sweatshirt

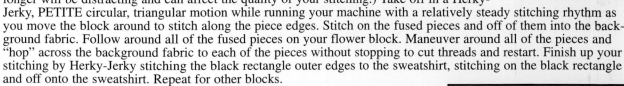

To complete your sweatshirt, cut off the bottom ribbing from the sweatshirt and fold up and pin a 1/2" hem to the <u>outside</u> of the shirt so the wrong side of the sweatshirt shows. Using Sulky 12 wt. Cotton #1005 Black, hand-stitch the hem in place with a 1/2" running stitch, or machine stitch with a long straight stitch or triple straight stitch. Turn down your neckline ribbing in half also to the outside and stitch as you did the hem.

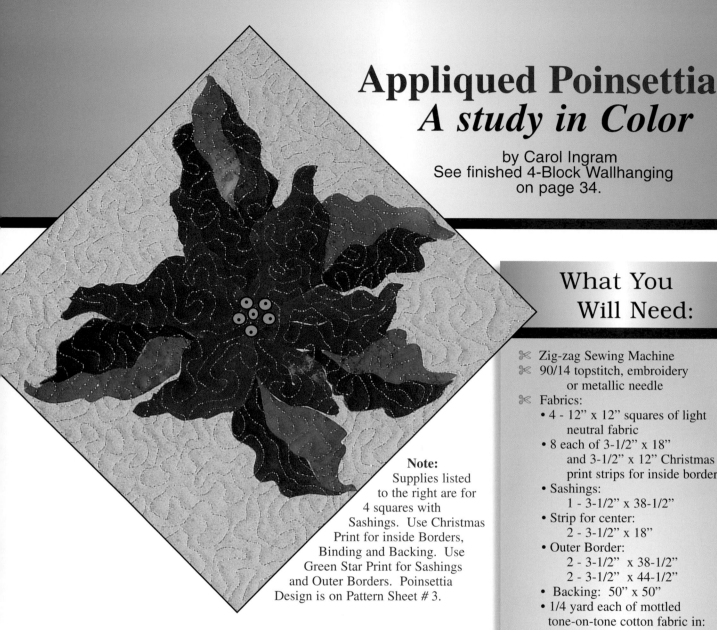

Appliqued Poinsettia
A study in Color

by Carol Ingram
See finished 4-Block Wallhanging
on page 34.

Note:
Supplies listed
to the right are for
4 squares with
Sashings. Use Christmas
Print for inside Borders,
Binding and Backing. Use
Green Star Print for Sashings
and Outer Borders. Poinsettia
Design is on Pattern Sheet # 3.

What You Will Need:

- Zig-zag Sewing Machine
- 90/14 topstitch, embroidery
  or metallic needle
- Fabrics:
  - 4 - 12" x 12" squares of light
    neutral fabric
  - 8 each of 3-1/2" x 18"
    and 3-1/2" x 12" Christmas
    print strips for inside borders
  - Sashings:
    1 - 3-1/2" x 38-1/2"
  - Strip for center:
    2 - 3-1/2" x 18"
  - Outer Border:
    2 - 3-1/2" x 38-1/2"
    2 - 3-1/2" x 44-1/2"
  - Backing: 50" x 50"
  - 1/4 yard each of mottled
    tone-on-tone cotton fabric in:
    Light Warm Red,
    Dark Cool Red,
    Light Warm Green, and
    Dark Cool Green
- Fusible Web
- 1 - 48" square of batting
- Regular sewing thread to match
- Sulky KK 2000 Temporary
  Spray Adhesive
- Sulky Rayon or Cotton Threads
  to match reds and greens
- Sulky Sliver™ or Holoshimmer™
  Metallic Thread in
  gold or silver
- Sulky Polyester Invisible Thread
- 2 - 9" x 10" squares of
  clear template plastic
- Scissors to cut template material
- Fine-line, permanent-ink marker
- Teflon Pressing Sheet
- Iron and pressing surface
- General Sewing Supplies

1 Get Fabrics Ready

1. Sew strips of a Christmas print around each of the neutral fabric squares. Fold each in half, then in half again and press to mark the centers of the neutral squares.

2. Apply fusible web to the wrong side of the two red and two green fabrics.

3. Using a fine-line, permanent-ink, black marker, trace two sets of the poinsettia patterns from Pattern Sheet #3 onto the quilter's template plastic material. Set one aside to use later as a placement guide, and cut the other on the traced lines.

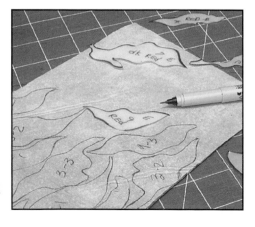

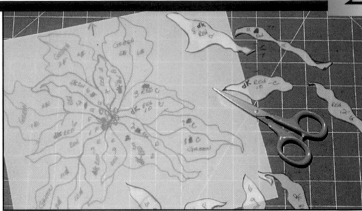

1. Reverse each template piece and lay them on the fusible web side of the fabrics; put pieces for warm petals on warm red and cool petals on cool red. Trace and cut out. Do the same for the green leaves.
2. Place uncut template in the center of the creased, prepared fabric. Arrange warm and cool reds alternately on the right and left sides of each flower to show contrast. A light warm red should lie next to a dark cool red on each petal. Do the same for the warm and cool greens for the leaves. Making the edges of each piece match exactly is neither important nor desirable since a tiny amount of the background fabric showing through gives depth to the finished poinsettia.
3. Once you are satisfied with the placement, carefully slide the plastic template out from under arrangement; iron the pieces in place.

Hint: For placement, if you are able to see through your background neutral fabric, you could slide the template under the fabric and not have to move your pieces later.

3   Layer, Quilt & Bind

1. Thread the machine with the Sulky Rayon or Sulky Cotton of your choice and do a decorative or small zig-zag stitch on the edges of each piece.
2. Sew the quilt squares together and add the outer borders.
3. Lay the backing wrong side up and spray with Sulky KK 2000. Place the batting over the backing. Spray the wrong side of the appliqued poinsettias with KK 2000 and place over the batting. Use a few pins to secure the corners through the quilting process.
4. Quilt as desired, using Sulky Sliver or Sulky Holoshimmer Thread through a 14/90 needle.
   Hint: Sulky Polyester Invisible Thread in the bobbin makes free-motion work with Sliver much smoother.
5. Bind and attach a hanger if desired.

Tip:

Stabilizer Tip from Martha Pullen, host of the PBS TV Show "Martha's Sewing Room"

1. When appliqueing on knits, turn the garment inside out and lay on a flat surface, making sure there are no wrinkles and it is relaxed (not stretched).
2. Spray lightly with KK 2000.
3. Place a piece of Soft 'n Sheer over area to be appliqued, making sure that the stabilizer is larger than the applique.
4. Spray again lightly with KK 2000 and place 1-2 layers of Tear-Easy Stabilizer over the Soft 'n Sheer.
5. Complete the applique.
6. Carefully remove the Tear-Easy Stabilizer, one layer at a time, so as not to distort the stitches.
7. Trim the Soft 'n Sheer close to the stitching, being careful not to cut the stitches. The Soft 'n Sheer remains on the inside of the design to continue stabilizing through washings.

Stained Glass Cutwork
Featuring Reverse Applique
and the New Sulky "Holoshimmer" Metallic Thread

Project can be done by computer embroidery method or using satin-stitch applique methods.

Nancy Cornwell
*Author, Speaker,
Fabric Designer for
David Textiles*

*Prior to 1999, Nancy owned a Stretch & Sew fabric store for 18 years. She has written the best-selling books **Adventures with Polarfleece, More Polarfleece Adventures**, and **Polar Magic**. She has been a contributing author in many sewing books, consumer magazines, and trade magazines. Nancy designs fabrics for David Textiles and is a sought-after speaker, presenting seminars nationally, and has been a guest on numerous sewing-related television programs.*

Nancy credits Mike and Molly, her precious kittens, for keeping a smile on her face when she experiments and tackles new ideas. They constantly involve themselves in all aspects of every project from rearranging pattern pieces on the cutting table to retrieving scraps from the wastebasket (just in case something happens to be in there by mistake!).

Project Overview

The snowflakes on this lovely fleece swing coat incorporate both cutwork and reverse applique techniques. The use of reverse applique lends a depth to the embellishment while the sheen of the accent fabric and the sparkle of Sulky Holoshimmer thread "dresses up" the fleece. The accent fabric chosen for the snowflakes is a poly satin that can be found in the bridal department of your local fabric store. (As long as the accent fabric is washable, like the fleece, it will work for the reverse Applique.)

"As soon as I felt the strength of Ultra Solvy, I knew it offered a terrific new (and much easier) way to do cutwork on fleece. It offers a way to trace and stitch-transfer motifs while simultaneously providing stabilization for the multiple stitching, trimming, and satin stitching steps. Simply moistening the Ultra Solvy turns it into an "adhesive stabilizer". Ultra Solvy stabilized the cut edges and acted as a topping for the new Sulky Holoshimmer satin stitching. Since no stabilizer remains in the stitching, it is perfect for those times when the wrong side of your embellishment will be visible. Especially wonderful when sewing fashion colors.

Thank you, Sulky, for listening to adventuresome sewers, and responding with a continual supply of innovative new products and techniques that help us with our creative endeavors. You encourage us to push beyond what fabrics and machines were intended to do. And the results are fascinating! And I love the new Sulky Holoshimmer Metallic thread. It was easy to sew with and added just the right pizazz to the snowflakes." --- Nancy

What You Will Need:

- ✂ Sewing Machine capable of computer embroidery
- ✂ Pattern: Stretch & Sew #1025
- ✂ Fabric: Nordic Fleece, Winter White: 3 to 3-1/8 yards
- ✂ Poly satin (washable): 1/4 yard (for snowflake accent and pocket lining)
- ✂ Regular sewing thread, cream (for construction)
- ✂ Sulky Holoshimmer Metallic thread, Gold # 6007 (for satin-stitched snowflakes)
- ✂ Sulky Original Metallic thread, #7007 Gold (bobbin thread for the snowflakes)

If your machine does not handle metallic thread in the bobbin, you may substitute Sulky Polyester Invisible Thread or a matching 40 wt. Sulky Rayon Thread.

- ✂ 80/12 universal needle
- ✂ 90/14 metallic needle (for embellishing stitching)
- ✂ Sulky Ultra Solvy Water Soluble Stabilizer
- ✂ Wavy blade rotary cutter
- ✂ Applique scissors
- ✂ Fine-line, permanent-ink marker
- ✂ General Sewing Supplies

Note: The stitching samples here are shown in contrasting colors of fleece, thread, and accent fabric for best visibility. Since Snowflake #1 is the most detailed, it is used for the samples.

Preparation

1. Cut out garment pieces per pattern directions. Embellishment is done on cut-out pieces before construction.

2. Using a fine-line, permanent-ink marker, trace two each of Snowflake #1, #2, and #3 from pattern sheet #2 onto 5-inch squares of Ultra Solvy. Trace only the solid lines. Do not trace the broken lines. Mark the right side of the traced Ultra Solvy (ink-drawn side) with a pin.

2   Arrange Traced Snowflakes

1. Lay the right front (as when wearing) on your cutting table with the wrong side of fleece facing up. *Hint: To determine wrong side, gently pull the cut hem edge. Fleece will curl to the wrong side.*
2. With the pinned side (ink-drawn side) facing up, arrange the traced snowflakes on the right front. Keep motifs at least 1 inch away from front edge, side, and lower edges, and 2 inches below the neck edge.
3. Use a dampened sponge to moisten the wrong side (unpinned side) of the traced Ultra Solvy and adhere it in place. Smooth with fingers to secure. Let dry.

Note: The Ultra Solvy on the top of the fleece provides the necessary stability for satin stitching the cut edges, plus it acts as a topping for smooth thread coverage in the satin stitching. Caution: Only slightly moisten the Ultra Solvy, it quickly becomes tacky enough to adhere. Don't rub, and smear the ink.

Tip:

Use a hair dryer on cool setting, or lay the moistened Ultra Solvy in front of a fan to help speed up the drying time. Make sure the Ultra Solvy does not feel damp, tacky, or spongy before proceeding. If the presser foot "grabs" instead of slides across the Ultra Solvy, it is not dry.

3   Straight Stitch

With regular sewing thread in the needle and bobbin, straight stitch the snowflake motifs with a normal tension setting and a stitch length of 2 mm. This "stitch transfers" the design so it is visible on the right side of the garment for embellishment stitching.

Tip:

Choose a bobbin thread color slightly different from the fleece color. This provides best visibility, yet is easily covered with the satin stitching.

4   Trim away Cutwork Areas

Trim away the cut-out areas (shaded areas on the templates), trimming close to the stitching lines. (For best visibility, trim from the "Ultra Solvy" side.) You will be encasing this edge with satin stitched Sulky Holoshimmer Metallic thread, so make sure this trim is close and accurate for good coverage.

5   Apply the Satin Accent

1. For each snowflake, cut a patch of satin accent fabric large enough to generously cover the cut-out area.

2. Slightly moisten the traced Ultra Solvy around the edge of the cut-out area and adhere the right side of the satin patch to the moistened Ultra Solvy. Let dry.

Be sure that the shiny side of the satin shows through the cut-out areas.

6   Add Ultra Solvy to the back

Snowflake #1:

For each snowflake, cut a patch of Ultra Solvy large enough to cover the entire snowflake area. Lay jacket front right side facing up. Moisten the Ultra Solvy patch and adhere it to the fleece, completely covering the design area. Allow the layers of Ultra Solvy to dry.

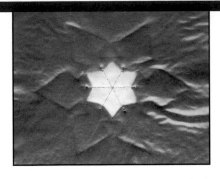

- Thread Machine Needle (size 90/14 Metallic Needle) with Sulky Holoshimmer Metallic Thread.
- Wind a bobbin with Sulky Original Metallic Thread #7007 Gold.
- Loosen top tension.   • Sew at a slow to medium speed.

Satin Stitch around the outside edge of each snowflake. This is not a pedal-to-the-metal operation. Sulky Holoshimmer Metallic Thread is a more delicate thread and performs better at a slower stitching speed. If you experience thread breakage and know that your needle is fresh, you are satin stitching too fast.

Using a 1.5mm straight stitch, stitch spokes of inner star, from inner point to inner point. Sink the needle 1/8" away from end of point and straight stitch across the satin to the point directly opposite. Repeat for the other two sets of points.

Satin stitch on a test sample of fleece, stabilized with adhered Ultra Solvy, to determine how much to loosen the top tension. Place the spool on the machine vertically so that the spool rotates as the thread is being pulled off. Set the tensions so that the Sulky Holoshimmer thread pulls slightly to the underside. Adjust stitch length for nice coverage without the stitches being too dense. "Too loose" is better than "too dense". A too dense satin stitch can cause distortion.

Snowflake Samples   8

2. From the wrong side, trim satin accent fabric close to the outer edges of the stitching lines. Use a 2mm stitch width to satin stitch the snowflake "spokes". Begin at one outer point and end at the opposing point. When stitching across the center spokes, cover the previous stitching lines.

1. Using a 3mm stitch width, satin stitch the edges of the cut-out areas. Make sure the swing of the zig-zag stitch goes completely over the cut edge of the fabric.

3. Use a 2mm stitch width to satin stitch the "V's" in the outer points, using the spokes as a pivoting point. The "V's" are shown as broken lines on the template. After you sew the first "V", lift the presser foot and slide over to the next lower "V".

Nancy's Quick Stitching Hint: Use your presser foot as a guide and stitch the first lower "V" a skimpy 1/4" above the bottom edge. No need to backtack since another satin stitching line will be covering the ends.

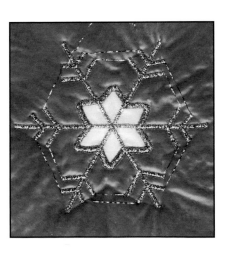

4. Continue around the snowflake until all six lower V's have been satin stitched. Repeat for the upper V's. When finished, clip all the jump threads on the right and wrong sides.

5. Depending upon the look you prefer, use either a 2mm width (green sample) or 3mm width (garment on page 104) and satin stitch the outer edges of the snowflake, making sure to cover all the spoke ends and "V" ends.

Snowflake #2:

Use a 3mm stitch width to satin stitch the edges of the cut-out areas. Make sure the swing of the zig-zag stitch goes completely over the cut edge of the fabric. From the wrong side, trim the satin accent fabric close to the outer edges of the stitching lines. Finish satin stitching the outer edges of the snowflake with a 3mm stitch.

Snowflake #3:

Stitch the inner spokes of the snowflake the same as snowflake #1. Use a 2mm stitch width to satin stitch over straight-stitched spokes. Begin and end 1/4" in the point ends. Using a 3mm stitch width, satin stitch the edges of the cut-out areas. Make sure the swing of the zig-zag stitch goes completely over the cut edge of the fabric. From the wrong side, trim the satin accent fabric close to the outer edges of the stitching lines. (If the accent fabric is adhered too firmly, trim after rinsing.)

9 Scarf Embellishment

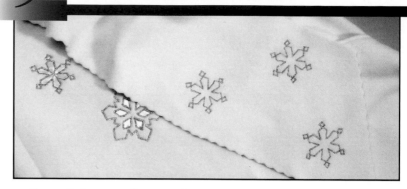

Snowflakes on the scarf are simply satin stitched motifs with no cutwork or applique.

Use a fine-line, permanent-ink marker to trace three #3 Snowflakes onto 5" squares of Ultra Solvy. Mark the right side of the traced Ultra Solvy (ink-drawn side) with a pin. Arrange the snowflakes on the right side of the right-angled edge of the scarf (as noted on garment pattern piece). With a dampened sponge, moisten the wrong side (unpinned side) of the traced Ultra Solvy and adhere it in place. Let dry. Use a 2mm width to satin stitch all of the snowflake's lines.

10 Construct the Garment

Ultra Solvy Removal:

Carefully cut away any excess Ultra Solvy that can **easily** be peeled away from the fleece. Do not try to peel off Solvy that has a strong hold. (You risk de-fleecing the fabric.) Soak the embellished snowflakes in cool water for 15 minutes. Rinse thoroughly several times, as necessary, until all the Ultra Solvy is gone. Roll in a towel and squeeze to remove the excess water. (Do not twist.) Lay flat to finish drying.

Garment construction:

Complete garment per pattern directions. Finish the front, bottom, sleeve, and scarf edges with a wave blade rotary cutter. Since the garment right front has essentially "been laundered" (with all the rinsing) and the rest of the garment has not, if the surface looks different from the rest of the garment, toss coat in the washer on gentle cycle and tumble dry on low.

For in-depth information on sewing fleece, refer to these Krause Publications by Nancy Cornwell.

The Oriental Lady
Draped Applique
A new look in applique

Lynn Dooly-Marek
Designer/Instructor

"I have been working with Sulky Threads for many years now; the color range is fabulous and the results are absolutely beautiful. Thank you, Sulky, for such an excellent product." --- Lynn

Lynn is a professional artist who loves to sew. Her paintings have won awards in both Canada and the U.S. She has worked with top Canadian designer Marilyn Brooks and has developed her own line of "original art-wear" designer jackets. A number of her paintings have been published as limited-edition prints and have been used on the covers of Reader's Digest and other publications. Lynn enjoys creating with quality fabrics and has pioneered a free-motion technique while designing appliques for her wallhangings and jackets. She works exclusively on the Husqvarna sewing machine. Lynn is the Canadian distributor for the San Francisco company, Sewing Workshop Pattern Collection.

Lynn's constant sewing companion is Cosmo, a 6.5 lb. Pomeranian. He is very educated and thoroughly enjoys the classical music that is constantly playing at home. He delights in sitting smack-dab in the middle of whatever fabric happens to be on the floor.

*Visit Lynn's website:
wwwynndoolymarek.com*

1 Preparing the Fabric

1. Cut your fabric 2-3" bigger all around than the actual garment pattern piece onto which the Oriental Lady will be appliqued. This allows for shrinkage due to "pulling" while appliqueing. Iron Sulky Totally Stable onto the back of the fabric. If the fabric is lightweight, add a layer of Sulky Tear-Easy by spraying it with KK 2000 and adhering it to the Totally Stable.
   No hoop is required.

2. From pattern sheet #2, use a fine-line, permanent-ink marker to trace the outline of the lady onto Sulky Solvy. (Spray with KK 2000 to eliminate shifting.)

3. Adhere Solvy to the right side of the fabric by spraying the fabric lightly with KK 2000 and smoothing the Solvy over the fabric.

Elsa Hopman from Sewing Machines Etcetera in Burlington, Ontario, Canada, created this rendition of the Oriental Lady in a class she took from Lynn. The closeup to the right shows alternative decorative stitching, creating swirls in addition to straight and satin stitched lines. Beautifully done.!

What You Will Need:

- ✂ Sewing Machine
- ✂ Sulky Totally Stable Iron-On Stabilizer
- ✂ Sulky Tear-Easy Stabilizer (Optional - unless using very lightweight fabric)
- ✂ Sulky Solvy Water Soluble Stabilizer
- ✂ Fine-Line, Permanent-Ink Marker
- ✂ Sulky KK 2000 Temporary Spray Adhesive
- ✂ Sulky Polyester Invisible Thread - clear for light fabrics, smoke for darker fabrics
- ✂ Sulky 30 wt. or 40 wt. Rayon Thread #1005 Black, #1039 True Red, #1165 Lt. Sky Blue and #1031 Med. Orchid
- ✂ Sulky Polyester Black Bobbin Thread
- ✂ Rayon or drapable fabrics for clothing. Background fabric - cotton or broadcloth of your choice. Small piece of white cotton for face, neck and hands.
- ✂ Q-Tips
- ✂ Garment or wallhanging pattern of your choice
- ✂ General Sewing Supplies

2 Stitch the Fabric

1. Using Sulky 40 wt. Rayon #1005 Black, free-motion straight stitch around the outside lines where the fabric is to go. This does not have to be precise.

2. Remove all of the Solvy by applying a wet Q-tip along the stitched lines to release the Solvy easily without dipping it in water.

3. Trace the face and neck outlines, and face details onto another small piece of Solvy. Spray the white fabric lightly with KK 2000 and place the Solvy on it. Cut out, leaving Solvy in place to stitch the face and neck details.

   Make sure the Oriental Lady is standing straight up - you don't want her crooked.

3 Free-Motion Embroider

Note: Unless otherwise directed, use Sulky 30 wt. or 40 wt. Rayon #1005 Black on the top and Black Sulky Polyester Bobbin thread in the bobbin throughout, and a straight stitch or a very narrow, open zig-zag.

Face and Neck: Carefully and slowly free-motion stitch all face and neck lines.

Hat and Hair: Trace pattern for hat and hair, and cut from black fabric. Spray with KK 2000 to hold in place. Stitch in place.

Lips: Outline in black first, then, using Sulky Rayon #1039 True Red, fill in the lips.

Eyes: Around outer corner edges of her eyes, use Sulky Rayon #1165 Lt. Sky Blue, and, further out above the eye, #1031 Med. Orchid. These colors do not go all the way around the eyes (see pattern sheet for details of face stitching).

Hands: Using the same fabric as for the face, trace and cut out hands. Free-motion stitch the lines of the hands. (The hands could be added later after the sleeves are stitched on, if desired.)

Collar pieces: Cut 4 long triangle shapes, about 1" x 5"; they do not have to be either even, perfect or symmetrical. Pin these down and tack them in place with Sulky Polyester Invisible Thread. Remove pins.

4 Draping & Bunching

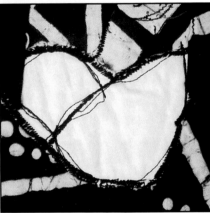

Clothing: Lynn recommends only natural fabrics for the clothing (silk, rayon, etc.) as they drape better. **Polyester will not drape properly.**

Draping and bunching: Cut an irregular shape of fabric approximately 12" x 12". Hold the bias ends so it is stretchy. Starting with her puffy sleeves, pin in place, following the lines that were stitched down originally. When you pin around the outlines, you usually end up with a pile in the middle. Flatten that pile, then pin the folds and creases in place. Press with an iron, if desired.

If you need additional fabric for the second sleeve, cut more. Bring the same sleeve material down on both sides of her body. Tack both sleeves in place with Sulky Polyester Smoke Invisible Thread or Black Sulky Rayon, being mindful not to sew over the pins. Remove any remaining pins. *Lynn says she sometimes ends up using 20 or 30 pins.*

5 Body Outfit

Body outfit: With a piece of fabric (different in texture from the sleeves), 20-25" long x 5-7" wide, depending on the length of your garment or wallhanging, put a "skirt" in place. Once again, fold within the lines originally traced with the free-motion stitching. Pin, tack in place as before, and remove pins. Just beneath her hands, put 2 little strips of fabric (same fabric as the collar pieces closest to her neck). At the bottom of the skirt, place an irregular shape of fabric, approximately 2" x 7", similar to what you used for the sleeves.

Since everything is tacked into place now, alternately use a zig-zag and straight stitch to sew pieces in place. Constantly move the material backwards and forwards. Don't try to make neat lines. Stitch lines outside of her body lines for interest. On the bunched areas, you can simply sew a close group of zig-zags or a bar-tack to hold down the various folds. You could end up with 15 bar-tacks (or dots) in different places on the bunched fabric.

Shapes: They do not have to be even, perfect or symmetrical. Pin these down and tack in place with Sulky Polyester Invisible Thread. Remove pins.

Hint: Do not try to make neat lines. Have fun --- this is no-stress applique! Add lines outside her body for interest.

6 Free-motion Work

Branches: For the branches in the background, stitch a loose satin stitch with a narrow to medium zig-zag, randomly changing the width as you go.

Flowers: To add interest, Lynn did some oval-shaped flowers with Sulky Rayon #1031 Medium Orchid among the branches using two, wide, side-by-side satin stitches.

Sign your piece with your name or just initials. Then, once everything is sewn in place, remove the stabilizer from the back. Press well. Cut out the exact pattern piece for your garment or wallhanging, keeping the lady centered or slightly to one side, and construct it according to pattern directions.

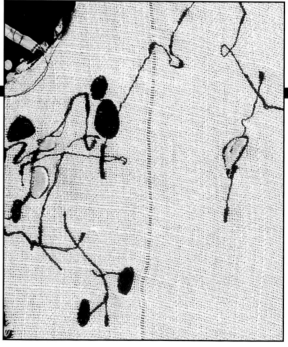

The Strolling Moose
Rag Wool™
Folk Art Applique

"The Sulky product line has become an integral part of the Rag Wool Embroidery™ technique. Sulky KK 2000 Temporary Spray Adhesive is an absolute must in every sewing room! The formula has the perfect amount of adhesive to aid in multiple tasks, and leaves no sticky residue. From template tracing to "cutlet" taming, KK 2000 has become my favorite sewing notion! Sulky Polyester Invisible Threads are the only threads that I will use for my technique because they can tolerate the heat of an iron without melting, which is critical for my technique! The choice of clear and smoke colors allows me to match the thread color to the wool, to make it truly invisible. Sulky Super Solvy Stabilizer is the perfect strength stabilizer for my Rag Wool Embroidery. It's strong enough to hold the "cutlets" in place, but washes away instantly! With availability in the various size rolls, I've found that hooping is quicker with minimal wastage." --- Kathy

Kathy MacMannis
*Owner of KMAC Embroidery
and Rag Wool Embroidery*

Kathy has been a sewing and craft enthusiast for as long as she can remember. In 1997, Kathy, intrigued with the concept of creating her own embroideries, purchased all of the accompanying software for her machine. Months of self-teaching paid off when she devised a technique that allowed her to manipulate the software programs to suit her needs. This expertise led to the beginning of KMAC Embroidery, which specializes in custom embroidery, and a career as a software educator.

In 1999, she created the Rag Wool Embroidery technique. Frustrated with the amount of time that hooking another rug would demand, she had a 2:00 A.M inspiration to use her embroidery machine to create the effect. Two hours later she had digitized and sewn out her first design, and knew she was onto something special! That inspiration has opened an entire new business for her. Kathy has taught at the International Husqvarna-Viking Convention and as a free-lance teacher around the country.

Kathy graduated from Simmons College with a B.S. in nursing, and still works as an emergency room nurse. She lives in Milford, MA, with her husband and their three children, who, along with their two cats, have been enlisted into the family business. "Max" and "Normar's" main purpose in life is to see how many cutlets they can spread throughout the house! The 100% wool clings to their fur, and it's obvious when mom has had a busy day in the workshop. They are probably the only cats in town with 100% wool coats.

Project Overview

Traditional rug hooking is a craft that typically takes hours to master and complete. With today's hectic schedules and demands, finding the time required to create these folk-art treasures is next to impossible. Although nothing can replace the beauty of a hand-hooked piece, this new three-dimensional technique called Rag Wool Embroidery™ offers an impressive alternative. The properties of the 100% wool fabric, along with the Sulky Invisible Thread, aid in creating this illusion. The "Strolling Moose" set of appliques offers a quick and fun way of creating this folk art illusion. These applique motifs are ideal for wearables and home decorating.

In order to felt properly, use only 100% wool fabric -- do not use blends. For all of the wool suggested for this project, try to include shades of each color for added interest, or use a hand-dyed, mottled wool with shade variations. The suggested dimensions can be a sum of multiple wool fabrics. Recycling from old clothing is perfect, as long as you know that it's 100% wool. If using recycled goods, wash first in hot water and put in the dryer. (If they are truly 100% wool, the material should be much tighter after drying.) Purchased wool fabric doesn't need to be prewashed.

What You Will Need:

- ✄ Sewing Machine with the capability of adjusting the presser foot pressure
- ✄ Darning foot or a clear presser foot
- ✄ Denim Machine needles size 14/90 or 16/100
- ✄ 1 "fat-sixteenth" or 9" x 14" medium to dark brown 100% wool for Moose
- ✄ 1-1/2 "fat-sixteenths" of gold 100% wool for the stars
- ✄ 1-1/2 "fat-sixteenths" med-dark green 100% wool for tree, shrub & grass
- ✄ 12" x 12" pieces of polyester felt: 2 gold, 2 dark green, 1 dark brown (felt should coordinate with the wool)
- ✄ Sulky KK 2000 Temporary Spray Adhesive
- ✄ Sulky Polyester Invisible Thread in both clear and smoke
- ✄ Sulky Super Solvy, either on the 12" roll or by the yard (1 yd. required)
- ✄ Rotary cutting supplies (mat, ruler, cutter)
- ✄ German wooden free-motion machine embroidery hoops, sizes 6-10"
- ✄ Fine-line, permanent-ink black marker
- ✄ Berber fleece jacket
   Optional: The "Strolling Moose" designs are also available on disk for owners of embroidery machines. They may be ordered at www.ragwool.com

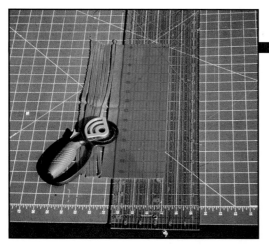

Preparing the Wool　　1

1. All of the wool will be prepared the same. For example, if you're using 3 shades of brown for the moose, those colors may be cut at the same time and mixed. Otherwise keep your wool colors separate.
2. Using your rotary cutting tools, cut 1/4" to 3/8" wide strips from the piece of wool fabric. You don't need to measure accurately; variation in size is just fine.
3. Take the strips of wool and lay them horizontally on the cutting mat. Cut the strips once again approximately 1/4" wide. What you've just created are hundreds of tiny bits of wool squares we'll call "cutlets".

2　Prepare the Sewing Patterns

1. Lightly spray the star pattern from pattern sheet #2 with Sulky KK 2000 Temporary Spray Adhesive and place a 12" x 12" piece of Super Solvy stabilizer over the pattern.
2. Using a fine-line, permanent-ink marker, trace the star outline and sewing lines of the pattern onto the Super Solvy.
   Note: Trace the smaller star twice.

1. Lightly spray the coordinating color of felt with KK 2000 Temporary Spray Adhesive. This really helps control the cutlets.
2. Scoop up a large pinch of cutlets and begin placing them in the center of the felt. Continue adding to the sides of the cutlet pile until the wool cutlets extend at least one inch beyond where the design will be sewn. Squish the pile down with your hand to compress the cutlets. Fill in areas that appear thin.
3. Steam press the pile of cutlets using an up and down motion.
   Note: The iron should be hot enough to steam, but not so hot that it will melt the polyester felt.
4. Lightly spray KK 2000 over the wool cutlets and the surrounding felt.
5. Place the Super Solvy with the traced design over the center of the cutlet pile.

Note: When sewing over dark colored wool, it may be beneficial to first place an unmarked piece of Super Solvy over the cutlet pile, followed by the Super Solvy with the traced design. Having two layers of Super Solvy creates a hazy appearance which makes it easier to see the lines. Spray KK-2000 between the layers of Super Solvy to prevent shifting.

Tip:

What you want to achieve is an area of wool that is approximately 3/8" thick and which will extend one inch beyond all sides of the template. The most important thing to remember is that there should be no holes or gaps where you can see the base fabric. To help prevent "air pockets", build your cutlets from the middle of the felt and work your way toward the outside.

Hoop the Cutlet Sandwich *4*

Tightly hoop the "cutlet sandwich" in an appropriate size German hard-wood hoop. The hoop should not be touching any of the cutlet pile, and should be large enough so there is at least one inch from the inside hoop edge to the pattern markings.

Tip:

When hooping for machine use, place the larger of the hoop rings down first, followed by the material, and then the top portion of the hoop. Lightly tug at all edges so that the "sandwich" is very taut.

5   Setting up the Sewing Machine

1. When sewing on something this thick, decrease the presser foot pressure in order for the applique to sew properly by gliding over the top of the "sandwich". Consult your machine's manual on how to make this adjustment.

2. Set the machine on straight stitch. Increase the stitch length a notch or two. Adjust this as needed while sewing if the stitches are too close together. Insert a "denim" needle size 14/90 or 16/100. A denim needle has a much stronger shaft. Place either a darning foot or a clear open-toe foot on your machine.
   Remember: The feed dogs should remain in the "up" position.

3. Thread the top with either clear or smoke Sulky Polyester Invisible Thread. Clear should be used on the lighter color wool, while the smoke works best on the darker fabrics. Using the wrong color does make a difference. Insert any color or type thread in the bobbin that contrasts with the felt to allow better visibility when it is time to cut out the applique. Decrease the upper thread tension by half. To determine if your tension is correct, sew a test piece. Take a scrap piece of felt and fold it several times to mimic the thickness of the cutlet sandwich. Sew through the layers. If there is bobbin thread being pulled to the top, the upper tension is too tight. Keep sewing and decreasing the upper tension until the bobbin thread is no longer visible. Record this number for later use.

Sewing the Applique Design   6

1. On the pattern, the starting position is marked. Always sew the outline first. If your machine has the option of needle position "up or down", set it to the down position because it is easier to pivot when the machine has stopped with the needle in the material. If the design contains inner or outer corners, backstitch at these places for added strength.

2. Sew the outline, backstitching several times at the beginning. Recheck your upper thread tension and your presser foot pressure as you stitch. You should be able to move the hoop freely, and the bobbin thread should not be visible.

3. After completing the outline, begin sewing the inner sewing lines. Always keep the line in front of you. As you're sewing, turn the hoop. When stopping to pivot, always stop with the needle in the material. If turning is difficult, lower the presser foot pressure some more. With just a little practice, you'll find that you are moving the hoop without even thinking about it. Try to focus your eyes not at the needle, but rather slightly in front of the presser foot.

4. Finish sewing the design, then backstitch several times.

Finishing the Design   7

1. Remove the hoop from the machine and carefully remove the **excess** Super Solvy from around the outer edges of the stitching. Brush away the excess cutlets that weren't sewn, and place them in a baggy for later use.

2. The remaining wool should be underneath the Super Solvy, but it will have various length cutlets protruding from the edges. With a sharp pair of scissors, redefine the outline by trimming the wool to within 1/8" to 1/4" of the outline. *Be very careful not to clip any of the design's threads.*

3. Under a running faucet, thoroughly wash away all of the Super Solvy, working the design with your fingers. It is very important to **completely** remove the Super Solvy. As the 100% wool absorbs the water, the wool will literally inflate.

4. Toss the finished design in the dryer for approximately 25 minutes or until dry, or the design may be air-dried.

5. Inspect the design for any areas where the base fabric may peek through. To fix any gaps: thread a hand needle with sewing thread, double the thread, and knot; from the back of the base fabric, bring the needle through to the top and thread a spare cutlet through its center onto the needle; take a small stitch back through the cutlet's center and through to the back of the fabric; pull the thread snugly to work the wool into the needed area; add as many spare cutlets as needed, then cut and tie off the thread; from the front, trim the added pieces of wool so they are the same height as the rest of the design.

6. With the felt side up, carefully cut out the applique using the contrasting bobbin thread as a guide; cut to within 2-3 millimeters of the outline. When you turn it over, no felt should be visible.

7. Repeat steps 1 through 7 on pages 114-117 for each design element, i.e., tree, moose, etc.

Applying the Appliques to the Jacket Back *8*

Two options to apply the applique:

Option 1: Use a straight stitch around the outside edge. The stitching line should fall 1/8" from the outside edge.

Or

Option 2: Use a buttonhole stitch or a blind hem stitch that will sew a couple of straight stitches on the garment and then swing to the left. Adjust the width of the swing so that it catches the applique.

Note: The "grass" applique can be treated as two separate elements, or sewn together to create one long piece.

1. When all of the designs are dry, lightly spray the appliques with KK 2000 and pin them to the jacket using the picture as a layout guide. You don't have to pin nearly as much when you have sprayed with KK 2000.

2. Depending on the wool color, thread your sewing machine with either clear or smoke Sulky Invisible Thread. Keep your top tension decreased for the monofilament thread so that you don't see the bobbin thread on top.

3. Once your garment is complete, future washings should be done with care. Hand wash and drip-dry all finished items. Mark and store a small baggy containing the various color cutlets used in the project for possible future repairs.

Tip:

Sulky KK 2000 Tip from Kaye Wood, host of the PBS TV Show, "Kaye Wood and Friends"

"I use Sulky KK 2000 in my new book, 'Pieces of Eight'. My "Applique with a Fray Technique" uses layers on a background square. Since many applique techniques use layering, I love using KK 2000 because it holds the layers in place, is repositionable, makes it easy to sew to the background, and it disappears without washing, so there is no added bulk. This is important when you are dealing with multiple layers." - - - Kaye Wood

Sources Information:

For those owning embroidery machines, the "Strolling Moose" designs are available in all embroidery machine formats. Rag Wool Embroidery design disks, kits, 100% wool cutlets, and hand-dyed wool may be ordered online at www.ragwool.com, or through: **KMAC Embroidery, 8 Daniel R. Drive, Milford MA 01757** - (508) 478-9526

Appliqued Sweatshirt
Stacked Chenille Applique using Prints

The Stacked Chenille came about when Leta and her friend, Rose Ford, started experimenting. After several failures, the technique was developed. The technique can be used as an applique or in whole garments like vests or jackets. The addition of embroidery, quilting and embellishment enhances an already appealing project.

Leta Myers
Free-Lance Instructor
Quartzsite, AZ

Leta and her husband, Vaughn, have lived in Quartzsite, AZ, since 1993. Prior to that, they lived in Alaska where they raised their family.

Like a lot of others, Leta started sewing as a child. Sewing doll clothes, crude as they were, sparked the love of sewing. Teaching is another love. She enjoys Machine Embroidery and Machine Arts Classes. Leta is a member of MEOW (Machine Embroiderers of Oregon and Washington) and CAME (California Association of Machine Embellishment). She is a Creative Stitches Certified Instructor. She also has attended the Husqvarna-Viking Convention for several years. She has taken every possible class and still it's just never enough.

She has taught classes from Alaska to Arizona. Living in the middle of the desert and having to drive eighty miles one way to teach, proves her devotion to her craft. Leta tries not to limit herself, and she is always looking for new techniques in any kind of machine art.

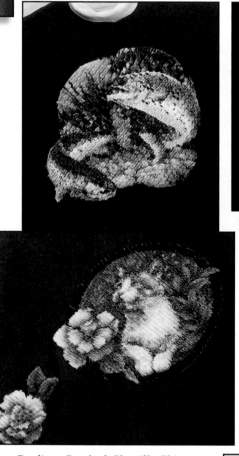

You'll need 4 fabric prints of any design. Any size print can be used. Graphic prints are best. All prints shown are by Springs Industries.

Credits: Stacked Chenille Shirts above created by Patti Lee. Horse Print by Leta Myers. They are all made following the steps on pages 119-120. "God Bless America" wording under the flag was machine stitched with two different colors of Sulky 12 wt. Cotton through a size 16/100 needle. The words were traced onto Ultra Solvy from the Pattern Sheet, and adhered in place with KK 2000. Using an Open-toe Applique foot, the words were stitched with a triple straight stitch. Remove Solvy and wear with pride!

1   Decide on a Print

Choose a design from fabric that will fray. Decide how much of the design that you wish to include in your stacked applique picture.
Hint: Unless the print is from a lightweight rayon or silk, you may want to choose a heavier weight garment to support the weight of 4 layers.

What You Will Need:

- ✄ Sewing machine with a walking foot and guide (optional)
- ✄ Sharp Scissors with blunt ends
- ✄ 24" Quilter's Ruler
- ✄ Pencil, chalk pencil, or water-soluble pen
- ✄ Clover™ Slash Cutter or Rotary Cutter and thin mat to slide in channels for cutting
- ✄ Sulky 30 wt. Cotton Thread for needle and bobbin
- ✄ Contrasting thread (optional)
- ✄ Base garment
- ✄ Fashion fabric with feature print - enough to layer 3 to 4 pattern repeats
- ✄ Sulky KK 2000 Temporary Spray Adhesive
- ✄ Sulky Polyester Invisible Thread
- ✄ General Sewing Supplies

2   Mark the Fabric

Mark the bias line on fabric using a water soluble or chalk marker. The drawn line represents the angle the chenille will flow.
Note: Chenille can be made to flow in either direction depending on what is happening in your selected print. The left to right forward movement of the horses dictated angle used.

3   Cut out the Design Area

Cut out the design 3 or 4 times, including all of the print that you want to show.

Tip:

If you use 4 layers and only cut 3, your design will be sharper. If you cut all 4 and use your garment as the base fabric, it will show lines of the garment and will not be as sharp. The bottom layer needs to be at least 1/2" larger all around than the others. This makes it easier to cut after it has been stitched.

Stack Layers, Pin, and Spray   4

Stack all the layers, being sure that the one with the bias line marked on it is on the top, and that the larger one on the bottom extends all around the perimeter just slightly. Using straight pins in several areas, line up the design, matching the exact same places on all layers. Pin together securely. Spray Sulky KK 2000 Temporary Spray Adhesive on the back of the chenille stack and apply it to your sweatshirt or whatever you wish to place the chenille on.

Match prints with pins.   **Spray wrong side of stack.**

5 Stitch the Channels

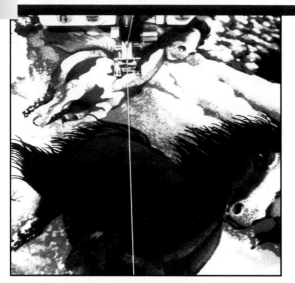

With a straight stitch length of 2 or 2.5, stitch along the drawn bias line using a matching Sulky 30 wt. Cotton Thread or sewing thread. Stitch parallel lines at equal distances apart out to the edge of the design. The lines can be from 1/4" to 1/2" apart. Continue with the same equal spacing throughout.

Hint: The closer the lines, the fluffier it will look. Leta's preference is 3/8". Using the presser foot width as a guide and adjusting the needle position is ideal.

Be sure to lock your stitches at the beginning and end of each row. Do not stitch over the larger margin of the bottom piece because this will be cut away when done and any overlapping stitches will need to be pulled out. *Note: The stack in this project is already on the garment or sweatshirt as a base.*

6 Cut the Channels Open

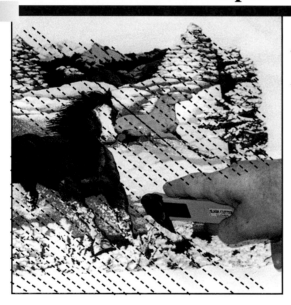

◄ *Note: We superimposed dash lines to indicate the stitched channels.*

After all lines have been stitched, cut between the stitched channels - **DO NOT CUT THE BASE LAYER**. Use either a *Clover Slash Cutter,* clipping about 1/2" of each channel before using; use a blunt-end scissors; or cut the layers with a regular rotary cutter but slide a thin line cutting mat by Omnigrid™ made especially for chenille work into the channel before cutting down to the appropriate layer. Carefully cut away the unstitched small margin that extends around the bottom piece.

7 Wash & Dry

After all the stitching and cutting is done, wash and dry to fluff the chenille. Fluffing will be best after several washings and dryings. Your garment is now ready to wear. *Enjoy!*

Chenille Applique
Adding Dimension to Chenille

"Sulky Solvy is what I recommend and choose for sewing applique onto chenille. It holds the nap of the chenille down and allows the Sulky Rayon or Sulky Polyester Invisible Threads to sew smoothly, and none of the chenille pokes up through the stitching."--- Ann

Ann Warren
Owner of Ann's Needle & Hook Depot
Franklin, NC

With a little more than a personal stash, her teaching, designing and writing experience, and a dream of 30 years, Ann's Needle & Hook Depot opened its doors in January, 1997. From the beginning, the chenille technique helped draw customers, as it was the first model made for display.

Ann's ideas now provide an abundance of inspiration with a diverse variety of wearable art models, quilt samples and gift items. Ann's customers have deemed the shop "The fun place to be". We've come a long way, baby!

Ann says, "We could change the shop's name to Zeke's Needle & Hook Depot. He runs the store and makes the world's greatest customer greeter. (Wal-Mart has nothin' over us!) This Yorkshire Terrier took charge when he arrived on the scene eight months ago and is now a very essential part of the business."

1 **Front Chenille Panels**

What You Will Need:

- ✄ Sewing Machine
- ✄ Machine embroidery needle 14/90
- ✄ Pattern: "The Panel Vest"
  Judy Bishop Collection
- ✄ Fabric: Follow pattern requirements for
  vest, View A, EXCEPT - Add 2-1/4
  yds. muslin to serve as the chenille base
  for the front panels and back.
- ✄ 2-3/4 yards Osnaburg for making the
  chenille. (Do not prewash fabrics)
- ✄ 1-1/2" strip of green fabric that will
  fringe well
- ✄ Assorted fabrics for applique features -
  Ann used Kona Bay oriental fabrics for
  her applique features and a Hoffman
  fabric as her background for the vest
- ✄ 8" German Hardwood Embroidery Hoop
- ✄ Sulky Ultra Solvy Water Soluble
  Stabilizer
- ✄ Sulky KK 2000 Temporary
  Spray Adhesive
- ✄ Sulky 40 wt. Rayon Thread
  (choice of colors to match appliques).
  To accent, Ann used Sulky Original
  Metallic #7004 Gold, and for the
  branch and leaf applique:
  Sulky 40 wt. Rayon Greens #1174
  Dark Pine Green, #1177 Avocado,
  #1104 Pastel Yellow Green, and
  Sulky UltraTwist Rayon #3004
- ✄ Sulky Black Bobbin Thread
- ✄ Sulky Polyester Invisible Thread
- ✄ Clear plastic ruler with 45° angle
- ✄ Water Soluble Pen
- ✄ Steam-A-Seam 2
- ✄ Small, sharp scissors or Clover®
  Slash Cutter for cutting chenille

1. Cut 2 muslin strips 6-1/2" x 25" for the base of front panels. Cut 4 Osnaburg strips on the BIAS 5-1/2" x 25".

2. Layer 2 Osnaburg strips centered right sides up on each front muslin base. Spray Sulky KK 2000 Temporary Spray Adhesive between layers. Using regular sewing thread to match the Osnaburg, on each set, stitch a vertical line across the 5-1/2" side. Using the presser foot as a guide, sew vertical lines 3/8" apart the entire 25" length. Adjust your needle position, if necessary, to achieve the 3/8" spacing.

3. Cut between stitching lines through the top two layers only, leaving the bottom layer uncut.
   Hint: Even though you can use a small, sharp scissors, it is easier on your hand if you use the Clover Chenille Slash Cutter, but clip about 1/2" of each channel with a sharp scissors before slashing.

4. Straight stitch around the outside edge of each piece on the Osnaburg to secure all 3 layers, keeping cut edges even. (This also keeps it from unraveling during the washing and drying process.)
   Hint: Stitching from the wrong side is easier - the cut edges don't fight you.

5. Cutting the top 2 layers on the BIAS allows you to stitch vertical rows of chenille, which will then be horizontal rows on the front panels. Use vest pattern to cut out one at a time. Do not forget to reverse pattern piece.

This flag applique was made from a combination of chenille strips, stacked chenille and plain fabric strips. Designed by Carol Ingram in memory of those lost Sept. 11, 2001. **FREE PATTERN AVAILABLE.** *Send a stamped, self-addressed, long envelope to:*
911 Free Pattern/Bk14
Sulky of America
3113 Broadpoint Dr.
Punta Gorda, FL
33983

2 Chenille Back

1. From vest back pattern, cut 1 muslin base 1" larger all around than pattern piece.
2. Cut 2 pieces of Osnaburg using the back pattern. Do not add the 1". (This helps when cutting between stitched lines.) With right sides facing up, layer Osnaburg to muslin base, spraying with KK 2000 between layers.
3. Use a water soluble marker to draw a vertical line on the top layer in the center of the back, from the neck to the bottom of the vest. Stitch the line.
4. With a clear ruler, align the 45° angle line on the stitched line and draw across the ruler to the edge of the vest. Flip ruler over and draw across the opposite line to form a "V".
5. Use the presser foot as a guide to sew lines 3/8" apart in the "V" shape across the entire vest back.
6. As before, cut between the lines through the top two layers, leaving the muslin base uncut. Be sure to clip completely through both layers and into "V" areas.
7. Again, to keep cut edges smooth and secure, straight stitch around the outside edges of the vest back on the edge of the osnaburg, keeping cut edges smooth.
8. Wash front and back pieces in warm water, using detergent and fabric softener; dry completely in the dryer. (Do this 2-3 times for best effect.)

Hint: If you accidentally cut through all 3 layers, add an appropriately sized piece of muslin behind the layered piece and stitch in place along the already-stitched channel lines. Magic!

3 Apply the Appliques

1. Cut out scenes or favorite appliques such as the oriental-look fabric which we have chosen for this project.
2. Use Steam-A-Seam 2 as directed on the package. Cut and place scenes on the chenille front panels and back as you choose.
3. Fringe 1/4" or so of both sides of a 1 to 1-1/2" wide strip of green fabric by pulling out cross grain threads. *Hint: To start the fringe, it's helpful to lift the cross grain thread using a straight pin.*
4. Tuck the fringed grass strip under the flowers and water area on the back of the vest before fusing the applique down.
5. Fuse thoroughly using a press cloth because the chenille is a napped fabric and harder to adhere to.
6. With Sulky Polyester Invisible Thread on top and Sulky Bobbin Thread in the bobbin, use a blanket stitch or small zig-zag stitch to applique the pieces.
7. Choose a Sulky 40 wt. Rayon or Sulky Metallic Thread to embellish your applique pieces. Ann used Sulky Original Metallic #7004 Gold (and a 14/90 needle) to accent the umbrellas, flowers, leaves, and the water area.

4 "Thread Paint" the Branch Applique

1. Trace the pattern for the branch and leaves from pattern sheet #1 onto a 10" square of Sulky Ultra Solvy. Hoop for machine embroidery in the 8" German wooden embroidery hoop. *Hint: To make pattern tracing easy, spray the pattern sheet lightly with Sulky KK 2000 and smooth the Ultra Solvy over it...no shifting or movement while you trace.*

2. Set up your machine for free-motion work by dropping the feed dogs, attaching the darning foot, and inserting a new 14/90 embroidery needle. Thread the top with Sulky UltraTwist #3004, and the bobbin with Sulky Black Bobbin Thread.

3. Using only a straight stitch, move the hoop from side-to-side, filling in the branch area. To establish the "grain" of the branch, keep the arrows lined up with the hole in the throat plate.

4. Leaves: Thread the top with Sulky 40 wt. Rayon #1174 Dark Pine Green. With the same side-to-side motion, loosely fill in the leaves following the direction of the arrows. Staying exactly on the line isn't important. Change to Sulky #2115 Vari-Pine Greens on top and add highlights and additional fill-in.

5. When you are pleased with the results, remove from the hoop. Cut away excess Ultra Solvy, leaving about 1/8" all around.

6. Spray the back of the applique with Sulky KK 2000 and place it on the chenille back in the upper left hand corner area. Using Sulky UltraTwist #3004 and Sulky Black Bobbin Thread, stitch the branch in place with a straight stitch moving casually down the center. Straight stitch along the edges of the branch for a "no-show applique". The remaining Ultra Solvy holds down the nap of the chenille for you and keeps it from poking through as you stitch.

7. Ann liked the look of 3-dimensional leaves so she just lightly stitched down her leaves. To achieve that look, use either Sulky Polyester Invisible or one of the green rayons to straight stitch down the center of the leaves, branching slightly towards the edges, but still allowing the edges to be loose and free.

8. Thoroughly rinse out the Ultra Solvy, blot the back of the vest in a towel and lay flat to dry.

5 Construct the Vest

1. Follow vest pattern directions to cut remaining pieces.
2. Ann used Sulky 30 wt. Rayon Multi-Color #2241 to free-motion stipple the vest pieces.
3. Assemble the vest and wear with pride!

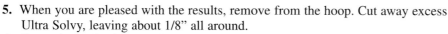

Battenberg Patchwork Fans
A Beautiful New Technique in Pieced Applique

"Sulky Tear-Easy Stabilizer has revolutionized our Battenberg Patchwork technique by allowing many of the designs to be completed as appliques. With the sheer, transparent construction of Tear-Easy, the design can be drawn directly onto the Tear-Easy, creating the pattern template. The patches are then fused to the pattern and the Tear-Easy becomes a permanent, lightweight backing for the applique." --- Dianna

Dianna Best
Author/Designer/Instructor

Born and raised in Hamilton, Ontario, Canada, Dianna now resides in Moose Jaw, Saskatchewan, Canada, with her husband and family. Dianna demonstrated an avid interest in sewing and needlework at a young age, so it was not surprising that she would pursue a career in this area. She received her education as a Home Economics Teacher at Ryerson Polytechnical Institute and the University of Toronto. Dianna has written and published a series of instructional books on Battenberg Lace and taught many workshops on this age-old needlework form in Canada, the USA and Australia. Her work has been on display at the Museum for Textiles in Toronto and her designs have been featured in needlework magazines. Dianna's continued work with Battenberg Lace has resulted in the development of a unique new technique she calls Battenberg Patchwork. With the release of her latest collection of Battenberg Patchwork patterns and the help of innovative new sewing aids from Sulky, Dianna has simplified the technique, making it easier than ever for sewers and quilters of all levels.

You can contact Dianna for more of her patterns at: dbest@battenberglace.com
Visit her web site: www.battenberglace.com
or CALL: 306-694-6052 FAX: 306-693-0431

1 Preparing the Fabrics

What You Will Need:

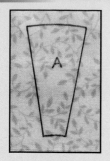

1. Apply a paper-backed fusible web to the wrong side of the patchwork fabrics following the manufacturer's directions. Remove paper backing.

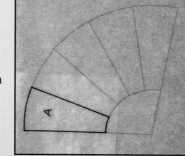

2. With a pencil, trace the fan design from Pattern Sheet #2 onto Sulky Tear-Easy. Cut a small piece of clear adhesive plastic (shelf liner) and remove paper backing.

What You Will Need:

- Zig-Zag Sewing Machine
- Sulky Tear-Easy Stabilizer - 5" square
- Sulky KK 2000
     Temporary Spray Adhesive
- Sulky Polyester Invisible Thread -
     Clear for light fabrics,
     Smoke for dark fabrics
- Sulky Sliver™ Metallic #8003 Gold
- Assorted Patchwork Fabrics (they can
     be as small as 1-1/2" x 2-1/2")
- 1/2 yd. of 1/4" Ecru Belgian Lace Tape
- Paper-Backed Fusible Web
- Clear Adhesive Plastic (shelf liner)
- Trims: i.e., buttons, charms, tassels
- No Fray Fabric Sealer
- Fine-Line, Permanent-Ink Marker
- Blunt Hand Sewing Needle
- Regular Lead Pencil
- General Sewing Supplies

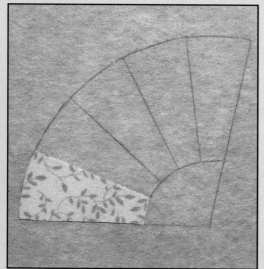

3. Position plastic (sticky side down) over space "A" on the Tear-Easy. With a fine-line, permanent-ink marker, trace an outline of space "A" onto the plastic, creating a template.

4. Remove template from Tear-Easy. To make an "easy pull-away point", place a tiny piece of paper under one corner of the outline as you position template onto right side of prepared patchwork fabric. Cut around outline leaving marker line on template. Starting at the "easy pull-away point", gently remove the template from the patchwork fabric.

5. Following manufacturer's directions, fuse this fabric patch to space "A" on the Tear-Easy. Repeat for remaining patches. Save the plastic template on waxed paper or release paper for use again.

2 Applying the Battenberg Tape

1. Cut lace tape as follows and apply fabric sealer to <u>one</u> end of each tape. **Tapes #1 to #5 - cut 2-1/2" for each. Tape #6 - cut a 13" piece.**

2. Beginning with the <u>sealed end</u>, center **Tape #1** over the junction of patches "A" and "B". Baste in place through the center of the tape. Reduce the top thread tension on the sewing machine. Using Sulky Polyester Invisible Thread on the top and Sulky Bobbin Thread, machine stitch along each edge of the tape. **Repeat for Tapes #2 through #4.** Trim excess tape length. Remove basting.

Note: While Dianna hand bastes through the center of the tape, you could lay tapes #1 through #4 on a brown paper grocery bag, spray them with KK 2000, and adhere them in place without basting.

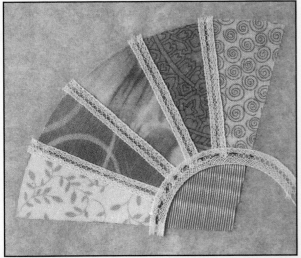

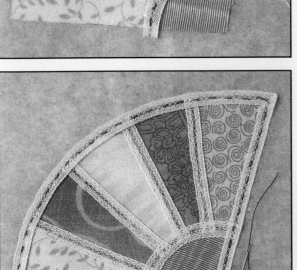

3. **Tape #5:** Beginning with the sealed end, center the tape over the small, curved, patchwork junction. Gently pull the "gimp" thread along the inner edge of the tape to shape the curve. The "gimp" thread is a coarse, whisker-like thread incorporated along each edge of the tape. Gently pulling this thread will cause the tape to softly curve, allowing the tape to be shaped to the design lines of the pattern. Baste the tape in place through the center of the tape. Machine stitch along both edges and trim off excess length.

4. **Tape #6:** Place the sealed end of the tape at the point of the fan, positioning it so that half of the tape is on the patchwork fabric and the other half is on the Tear-Easy. Begin basting 1/2" from the sealed end. At the corner, fold the tape back on itself allowing 1/8" to extend above the top of the fan. Securing the outer corner of the tape with your needle, lift, fold and pivot the tape creating a mitered corner. (See illustration below.)

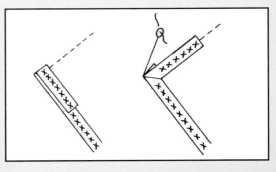

5. Secure corner with a basting stitch. Continue basting as you gently pull the "gimp" thread to maneuver the curve across the top of the fan. As you approach the point of the fan again, trim off excess tape length, allowing 1/4" for finishing. Apply fabric sealer and allow to dry thoroughly. Turn sealed end under, incorporating the starting end, and tack in place with a basting stitch. Machine stitch along the inner edge of the tape as close to the "gimp" thread as possible.

Embellish with Sulky Sliver *3*

Cut four 36" lengths of Sulky Sliver #8003 Gold. With the iron set on the lowest heat setting, lightly press thread to straighten. Thread the four strands through the eye of a blunt hand sewing needle. Double the threads and secure the ends with a knot. Bring the needle up through the patchwork from the underside, coming out at the base of Tape #1. Weave the thread over and under each of the X's in the center of the tape. Finish by bringing the needle to the underside again and secure the thread with a knot. Add Sliver to each of the remaining tapes. *This creates a really dramatic metallic finish!*

 # Remove the Stabilizer

Carefully tear away the stabilizer from around the fan. With regular sewing thread matching the fan, sew the fan applique to the garment or accessory of your choice. Embellish with buttons, charms, tassels, etc. For an added dimension, "puff" the fan by inserting a layer of poly fleece between the fan and the background fabric.

Make a Fan Ornament: Make two fan appliques as described above. Place them back to back with a double layer of poly fleece in between. Pin the layers together. Using Sulky Invisible Thread, whip stitch by hand (or machine stitch using a small zig-zag) around the outside edge. Leave open at the point for inserting the tassel.
Add decorative trims and a thread hanger at the top.

A Primary Clown Wallhanging

Make an overlay pattern using Sulky Ultra Solvy™ for easy applique placement

Designed by Joyce Drexler and presented on the PBS TV Quilting Show, "Quilts Central" with co-host Donna Wilder.

This happy-go-lucky clown applique could add his smiling face to clothing as well as pillows, throws or a wallhanging for any child's room.

The clown design was adapted from a fabric print collection by Donna Wilder's "Free Spirit"™ Fabric Company.

Delight your child or grandchild with this bright, easy to do applique! Let your child wake up to a smile everyday!

Make it today!

What You Will Need:

- ✂ Sewing Machine with an open-toe
     Applique Foot
- ✂ Sulky Ultra Solvy™ - 12" Roll
- ✂ Sulky KK 2000™ Temporary
     Spray Adhesive
- ✂ Fine-line, permanent-ink black marker
- ✂ Sulky 30 wt. Primary Color Threads
- ✂ Sulky Totally Stable Iron-on Stabilizer
- ✂ Sulky Polyester Invisible Thread
- ✂ Quilter's 24" Ruler, Rotary Cutter and Mat
- ✂ Iron-on Fusible Web with Release Sheet
- ✂ Iron, Press Cloth and Pressing Surface
- ✂ General Sewing Supplies - Pins, Scissors, etc.

- ✂ Fabrics: "Free Spirit's" Clown Coordinates
     1-1/2 yd. of Clown Blocks
        if spelling out "Smile" with them
        as well as using them as a Border
     For off-set Checkerboard Borders:
        1/4 yd. of Primary Blue
        1/4 yd. of Dark Blue Print
        1/4 yd. of Primary Yellow
        1/4 yd. of Primary Red
     Fat Quarters of Solid White and Red
     Fat Quarters of 5 Coordinating Prints
        for Clown Clothes
     1/2 yd. for 5th Outer Border
     3/4 yd. of Blue Print for Binding
        and Cornerstone Blocks
     1 yd. of Primary Stripes - cut on bias
     1/4 yd. of small Checks for 3rd Border
     5/8 yd. of Primary Mottled Blue
        for foundation Block for Clown
     1-1/4 yd. for Backing
     Batting

1 Prepare the Applique Fabrics

1. Following the Clown Design on Pattern Sheet #2, generously cut fabric pieces at least 1/2" larger all around than each applique area. From the block fabric print, cut out Blocks for the Clown to juggle.

2. Since the clown is symmetrical, there is no need to reverse the Clown Pattern. With a permanent-ink, fine-line black marker, trace the separate colored parts of the clown onto the paper release sheet of the fusible web.

3. Iron them onto the appropriate fabrics, following the layout on the photo of the finished clown on page 128.

4. Cut out designs on the drawn line, making sure your cut edges are smooth.

2 Solvy Overlay

1. From a 12" wide roll of Ultra Solvy, cut a length that is longer than the clown pattern and trace the clown pattern onto it. Moisten the top edge of the unmarked side of the Ultra Solvy pattern by lightly wiping over it with a damp paper towel; place it over the blue background fabric.

   Use this Ultra Solvy pattern as an overlay to help you place the clown pieces. Keep the top edge attached at all times and lift up the rest slightly to place pieces under it.

2. Spray the back of each piece with KK 2000 before putting it in place. Place the feet of the clown 3-1/2" up from the bottom and centered from left to right. Butt edges of the applique pieces together. Place letter blocks above the clown spelling out S-M-I-L-E.

3 Applique the Design

1. Look closely at the photo of the finished clown on page 128 to note that all of the corners where satin-stitched lines meet are squared off, not mitered. Choose the corner method you most prefer. Follow numbers for stitching order. Also, a double line may be used as we did where the hand meets the shirt. You might find that decorative stitches in combinations would also be cute.

2. Apply Sulky Totally Stable Iron-on Stabilizer to the back of the blue fabric. Stitch the Blocks with contrasting primary colors of Sulky 30 wt. Cotton or Rayon Thread. Use an open-toe applique foot. Reduce the top tension slightly for a softer looking satin stitch. Applique all of the pieces.

3. Trace the facial features onto a small piece of the Ultra Solvy. Dampen it with a moist paper towel and finger press it over a small piece of the face fabric. Let dry. Stitch the facial features with tapered satin stitches. Remove the Solvy.

4. Add borders; cut strips on the bias to get a spiraled look. Spray KK 2000 between layers of quilt top, batting and backing. Quilt with Sulky Thread. Bind.

Frayed Print Upside Down Applique
Using Sulky's New Holoshimmer™
in Red, Silver/White & Blue
Designed by Carol Ingram

What an easy way to show your colors! --- Make it tonight!

1. Choose your favorite USA Flag Print.
2. Carol chose a combination of prints that she cut apart and repositioned to applique this child's ready-made sweatshirt. Trim your print for placement, leaving a 3/4" seam allowance all around the outside edges.

3. Turn the sweatshirt inside out and place your trimmed flag print **RIGHT SIDE DOWN** on the **INSIDE** of the sweatshirt. To hold it in place, spray a little KK 2000 on the right side of the print on the seam allowance areas only.

4. Using regular sewing thread on top and Sulky Invisible Thread in the bobbin, straight stitch from the back, along all the design lines, i.e., around the star and down the stripes.
5. Spray KK 2000 on a sheet of Sulky Tear-Easy and place it over the back of the print on the inside of the sweatshirt. Turn sweatshirt right side out.
6. Thread the top with Sulky Holoshimmer #6045 Multi-color, and the bobbin with a Sulky 40 wt. Rayon to match the sweatshirt. Choose an appropriate decorative stitch like the starburst stitch that Carol used.
7. From the right side, stitch over all of the straight stitch lines.
8. *Carefully cut away within 1/4" of the stitching, all of the top sweatshirt layer covering the Star shapes and the Stripes print. Carefully clip notches in the remaining 1/4" to create a frayed look.*
   Wear with pride!

3-D Butterflies & Flowers
Special Effects in Dimensional Applique
using Sulky Water Soluble Stabilizer

Trish Liden
National Sulky "Sew Exciting" Educator

Creative stitching and Textile Art are an integral part of Trish's background. She earned a Bachelor's Degree in Home Economics with an emphasis on Clothing/Textiles/Art. She attends continuing education classes to maintain her status as a Certified Home Economist and enthusiastically welcomes opportunities to learn from others in the industry.

Prior to becoming a National Sulky Educator, Trish taught at a well-established sewing machine dealership and fabric/quilt shop in Southern California. She has been a four-term officer of her local Quilt Guild.

She loves to pass her enthusiasm for "exploration" of fabric and art to her students to inspire "the artist within". Trish believes that stitching enthusiasts are some of the most friendly, sharing people in the world. It is her pleasure to meet with them and to teach (and learn from) those who share her love of creative sewing.

This jacket and capri pants (McCall's #3135) outfit is modeled by Amber Drexler (age 10). Trish also added a cute fabric-covered headband to match! The high contrast between tinted colors and black/white make the simple shapes stand out dramatically.

Project Overview

"See spots and butterflies: Designing elegant, wearable art is a passion of mine. This book was the perfect opportunity to create wearable 'fun' for the younger set. Several Sulky stabilizers worked very well for this project. I used Cut-Away Soft 'n Sheer inside the jacket for soft support behind the flower and butterflies and mid-weight Super Solvy provided an excellent stitching surface for the stained glass cutwork butterfly." --- Trish

1 Flower

1. Using a white chalk marker, mark position of the stem and leaf appliques where you want to put them on the jacket print. Spray Sulky KK 2000 Temporary Spray Adhesive onto Sulky Soft 'n Sheer and position it on the inside of the jacket in the area behind the applique.

2. **Leaves:** "Crinkle" green leaf fabric by spraying starch onto it and arranging the dampened fabric into folds. "Set the crinkles" by ironing the fabric dry, then cut out 2 leaves. Position the leaves in place with KK 2000. Select a matching Sulky Rayon thread to free-motion stitch the vein lines in the leaves. (This is a raw-edge technique. Edges will softly fray and add interest.)

What You Will Need:

- ✂ Sewing Machine with blind-hem stitch
- ✂ Sulky Soft 'n Sheer Permanent Stabilizer
- ✂ Sulky Super Solvy Water Soluble Stabilizer
- ✂ Sulky KK 2000 Temporary Spray Adhesive
- ✂ Sulky Rayon Threads
- ✂ Various Applique Fabrics
- ✂ Pattern of your choice and fabric amounts per pattern, or use a ready-made jacket and capri pants
- ✂ White Chalk Marker
- ✂ Washable or Air-Erasable Marker
- ✂ Spray Starch
- ✂ Steam-a-Seam 2™ Fusible Web
- ✂ 8" or 10" German Wooden Machine Embroidery Hoop
- ✂ Sharp, pointed Scissors
- ✂ Template Plastic
- ✂ Pinking Shears - *optional*
- ✂ General Sewing Supplies

See Pattern Sheet # 2 for leaf, flower, butterfly and richelieu patterns.

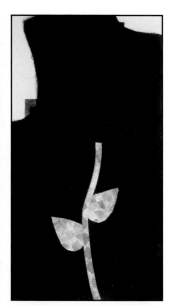

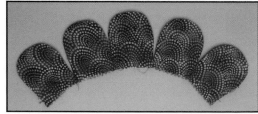

3. **Stem:** From the green fabric, cut a bias strip 3/4" wide by approximately 11" long. Turn under and iron both 11" raw edges making it about 3/8" wide finished. Lay the stem on the white chalk line, covering the bottom edge of the stitched leaves. Use a matching Sulky 40 wt. Rayon and a blanket stitch set at 2.0 stitch length to stitch all around the stem.

4. **Flowers:** Spray KK 2000 on the right side of one of two flower fabrics (one for the right side and one for the wrong side), and place it over the right side of the second flower fabric. Trace and cut out 5 petals. With right sides together, stitch all around the sides and top of each petal with a scant 1/4" seam allowance. Trim away most of the seam allowance with pinking shears. Turn petals to the right side and press. To connect all of the petals, line them up and stitch two rows of basting stitches 1/8" apart along all of the raw edge bottoms, 1/4" from the bottom. Gather the basting threads to form a tight circle of petals. Place the center over the top of the stem and stitch the flower in place using a decorative button center.

132

2 Finishes

1. **Playful finishes**: Trish found a cute, polka-dot button for the flower center and she embellished the flower with loops of Sulky Opalescent Sliver Metallic #8040 and Sulky Rayon Thread #1135 Pastel Yellow.

3 Small Butterflies

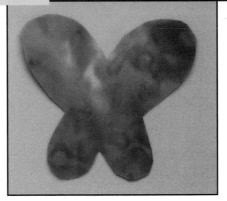

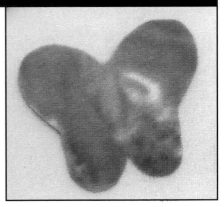

1. **Small butterflies:** Using Steam-A-Seam 2 (or other fusible web), fuse two matching WRONG SIDES together of 2 or 3 different fabrics, so that you have reversible butterflies. Trace the butterflies onto template plastic and cut out. Use the small template to cut out the shape. (Prepare a number of shapes to be sewn in the hoop at the same time.)

2. Cut 2 squares of Sulky Super Solvy approximately 1-1/2" wider than the German wooden hoop. Position one piece of Super Solvy over the adjustable outer hoop. Arrange butterflies on top. Place a second piece of Super Solvy on top and press down on the inner hoop. This forms a taut surface for the 3-D applique technique.

4 Large Butterfly

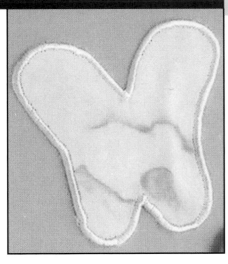

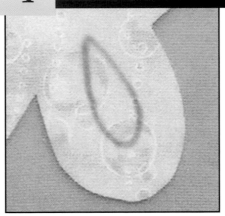

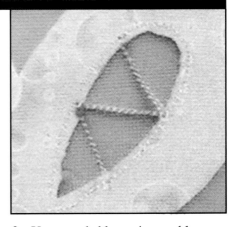

3. Thread the top and bobbin with a matching Sulky Rayon Thread and use a small satin stitch approximately 2.3 mm wide. Start at the "head" end of the center of each butterfly shape and satin stitch around the edges. Threads will wrap over the fabric for a beautiful finish. Shapes can be "punched out" (paper-doll style). Remove any left-over Super Solvy. Set aside for further embellishment.

1. **Cutwork (large) butterfly & 2-color underwing:** Using directions for small butterflies, fuse 2 fabrics, wrong sides together for the underwing, and 2 fabrics right sides together for the large outer butterfly. To make a 2-color underwing, cut an extra upper half of the butterfly wings in a contrasting color and fuse to one right side of the fused sandwich. Using the medium-sized template, cut out one underwing, keeping the contrasting fabric as a little more than 1/2 of the upper wings. Cut outer edge of large butterfly. **DO NOT CUT INNER WING DETAIL YET.** Satin Stitch the outlines as in #3 - Small Butterflies.

2. Use a washable or air-erasable marker to draw the cutwork shapes onto the Sulky Super Solvy.

3. With matching Sulky Rayon Thread in the needle and bobbin, straight stitch 2 or 3 times on the drawn lines through all layers on each butterfly. Remove the hoop from the machine *(keeping the work taut).* **CAREFULLY** cut out just the top layer of Super Solvy and the fused butterfly fabric within the cut work area.

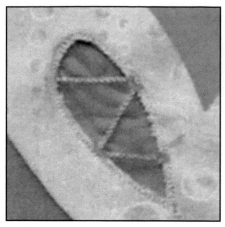

6. Change to a 1.5 width and satin stitch over the original satin stitches where the "reinforcement lines" connect. Change to a 2.3 width and satin stitch all of the cutwork edges again using the matching Sulky 40 wt. Rayon.

7. Remove from hoop and cut away the Super Solvy approximately 1/4" away from the finished butterfly shape. Soak in water to remove the remaining Super Solvy. Air dry, then press.

4. Draw the "richelieu" bars onto the Super Solvy cutwork. Put the hoop back in the machine.

5. Sulky #1005 black thread was used for the "stained glass" cutwork look on the larger butterfly below even though photos above show richelieu bars stitched with a matching color. Use a short 2.0 length and straight stitch on the lines several times. To reinforce the cutwork bars, connect them into the satin stitches as you stitch back and forth across the Super Solvy cut work.

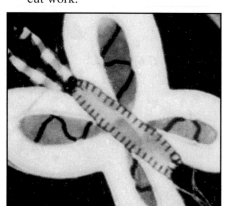

Tip:

Special Sulky Solvy Tips from Sue Hausmann, Host of the PBS TV Show "America Sews with Sue Hausmann"

"I save in a container, all the scraps of all weights of Solvy that I trim off projects before removing the last little bit either with a mist of water or by soaking the project in a sink full of water. Then when I need a 'paint-on stabilizer' to stiffen special projects, I just add water to the scraps to dissolve them. To save the left-over 'Solvy' liquid for the next project, put a lid on the container and keep it in the refrigerator. Label it of course.

Next time you purchase a pair of shoes or a small appliance, save the little package of 'silica' that comes in it. Store it with your Solvy stabilizers. The 'silica pack' absorbs moisture and will keep the open Solvy drier and firmer." --- Sue

8. Body: Select a contrasting fabric color and cut a strip approximately 3/4" wide x 4" long. Press edges under to the center to a finished size of approximately 3/8" wide. Twist one end of the strip and tuck it under the bottom (tail section) of the butterfly. Position the small butterfly (or larger butterfly and the colorful underwing) on the garment. It may be necessary to use a small strip of Sulky Soft 'n Sheer to stabilize the applique from the inside of the garment. Lay the strip to the "head" section. Black Sulky Rayon Thread was used to blanket stitch the butterfly body through the wing unit while attaching it to the garment. When finished, tie a knot which becomes the head. Leave approximately 3/8" and cut off the remaining portion of the strip.

6 Headband

Headband: A purchased headband was covered with leftover fabric from the capri pants. A small butterfly sits on top.

5 Details

Have fun! Add beads, knotted pieces of thread to flow from the butterfly body, gold antennae or more.

134

Child's Bath Caddy
Applique over Netting

Lindee Goodall
Co-Owner of
Cactus Punch®
Digitizing and Embroidery

Lindee Goodall is an international instructor, author, designer and founder/president of Cactus Punch. She has been a guest on the PBS TV shows Quilting from the Heartland, Martha's Sewing Room, and America Sews with Sue Hausmann. Lindee has authored numerous articles on embroidery and digitizing (Stitches, EMB, Home EMB, The Profitable Embroiderer, Impressions, Sew Beautiful, Sew News, Threads). Her love of sewing, degree in art, and experience as a programmer, technical instructor, and crafter led her to become a digitizer and commercial embroiderer. She started Cactus Punch in 1995 to create innovative and original designs for both home and commercial embroiderers. She and her husband, Bill, co-own and operate the company, which is located in Tucson, AZ. In 1997 Lindee won "Best Original Digitized Design" at METS and was named a "Digitizer of Distinction" by Impressions Magazine. She is also a skilled web designer, database developer, and a PADI Dive Master.

Her website is: www.cactuspunch.com

About my pets: "Cheyenne, the Sheltie, is my little girl while Rufus, an ornery yet loving cat, is my boy. Rufus likes to shove things on the floor and pull the threads off the racks." - Lindee

Ethan Noe is really enjoying playing in the bubble bath with all of his foam toys. And his Mom likes being able to put them up to dry in this bath caddy when his bath is done.

Project Overview

This child's bath caddy features embroidery on fish net. Embroidery can be performed on just about anything, provided you make a good design choice and you know how to prepare the fabric for embroidery. In this case, an applique design is the perfect choice. Terry cloth and fish net can be difficult, but for totally different reasons. While the fish net doesn't have enough fabric, terry cloth has, in a sense, too much. The loopy, thick texture of terry cloth is not always totally restrained by embroidery. Over repeated launderings, loops can work their way through embroidery unless a permanent topping is used. However, applique is also a perfect way to tame terry cloth. To give variety to our project, we'll applique the fish net with embroidery designs and we'll use free-motion applique for the terry cloth.

While we are making a child's bath caddy in this project, you can easily adapt this to a more adult or elegant theme by changing the fabrics and the appliques. For example, a lingerie organizer could be made using satin and silk fabrics, delicate floral motifs, and the techniques learned from embroidering on the fish net in this project. Think of this as a learning technique that you can apply to other projects.

What You Will Need:

- ✄ 1 large bath towel
- ✄ 5 contrasting 4" squares of applique fabric
- ✄ 5 - 4" squares of Steam-A-Seam 2
- ✄ Sulky 40 wt. Rayon Thread to match applique fabric
- ✄ Sulky 40 wt. #1005 Black
- ✄ Sulky 40 wt. #1001 White
- ✄ 1 - 14" x 20" Multi-color fabric for wave (can be pieced together)
- ✄ 1 - 14" x 20" Pattern Ease™ for wave template
- ✄ 1 - 4" x (width of towel + 6")
- ✄ 1 - 18" x 22" piece of fish net
- ✄ 2 - 18" x 22" pieces of Super Solvy or 1 piece of Ultra Solvy
- ✄ 2 - 8" x 10" pieces of Sulky Soft 'n Sheer Cut-Away Stabilizer
- ✄ 5 - 6" x 8" index cards
- ✄ Printed wave template (paper) *(see Pattern Sheet #4)*
- ✄ Quilter's Template Plastic
- ✄ 1 adult size plastic tubular hanger
- ✄ 1 - 20" x 20" piece of white cotton fabric for hanger pocket
- ✄ 1 yd. 1/4" elastic
- ✄ 4 packages of purchased, extra-wide, double-fold bias tape
- ✄ 2 safety pins
- ✄ Cactus Punch Embroidery Card: 1 APL01- Baby Sea Critters A-Z Appliques

1 Preparing the Fish Net

1. The fish net must be stiffened for embroidery. Sandwich it **between** two layers of Super Solvy or **under** 1 layer of Ultra Solvy.

   Make sure that the fish net is carefully arranged in a neutral (not stretched) position and that it is straight, and it will remain undisturbed until it is fully dry.

2. Either spray, mist, sprinkle or otherwise wet down the fish net so the Solvy is fully wet but not in a puddle. The object is for the saturated Solvy to soak into the fabric so that, when the fabric dries, it will be stiff.

   Due to the open weave of the fish net, spray-on fabric stiffeners do not work well. The fish net should be stiff and dry before use.

3. A hair dryer may be used to speed drying.Lindee laid hers out to dry on the floor of the shower in a spare bathroom; cake drying racks also work well if you are working at home.

Cut The Towels

1. To some degree, the size of your pockets and organizer will depend on the size of your towel. Refer to Figure 1 for the cutting layout. The width is based on your hanger. Measure the length by cutting through the decorative woven band (non-terry area) at the opposite end of the towel. While this area is not as thick, it is useful for the middle pocket, as you will see later.

2. To shape the caddy foundation, lay the hanger at the top of the towel as illustrated and trace the slope of the hanger (dotted line on illustration). Cut towel on the traced line.

3. Curving the lower corners will make it easier to apply the seam binding later. To get matching curves on each side, fold the towel in half vertically before cutting the curves.

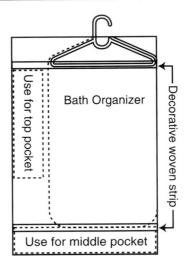

Fig. 1. Shape caddy by cutting on dotted lines.

Make the Applique Templates for Machine Embroidery

There are several ways to make appliques for machine embroidery. One is to take a piece of fabric, allow the computerized design to straight stitch the applique fabric down to the base fabric, then trim away the excess fabric. Lindee prefers this method when working with fabrics such as chiffon.

For cottons and other fabrics that have some body, she prefers the template method. Since this method is not as intuitive as the first (but more suitable for intricate shapes), we will use this method to create the template for our appliques.

1. Tape a 6" x 8" index card to the bottom of your hoop.

2. Insert the hoop into the machine and select the applique design.

3. Sew color 1 without any thread. The needle will perforate the card stock, providing an exact outline of the fabric you need to cut for your applique embroidery.

4. Remove the hoop from the machine. Write the name of the design within the perforations, and an arrow indicating the top of the design. Remove the index card from the hoop.

5. Cut out the template carefully, exactly following the needle perforations for accuracy!

6. Remove one paper from the Steam-A-Seam 2 and apply the fusible to the back of the applique fabric. Place the cut-out applique index card template *face down* on the Steam-A Seam and trace around the shape. Carefully cut out the shape. Precise cutting will result in a perfect applique.

4   Apply Appliques to Fish Net

Tip 1:

Since fish net offers very little fabric area to support the embroidery, you will need to sandwich it between a permanent backing and the applique. Since you will put two appliques on the shower caddy, determine the center position for each by dividing the width of the fish net into quarters (refer to fig. 2 on page 139).

1. Hoop fish net with Sulky Soft 'n Sheer cut-away stabilizer under it. While your fabric feels very stable now, it won't be once you wash out the Solvy, so a permanent backing is needed to support the stitches where there is no fish net fabric.

2. Go back to the beginning of the design. (Just go backward one color by touching in the color area, or select the design from the menu.)

3. At the location on the fish net where you want to place your first applique, center the design vertically in the space and sew the outline of the design with color 1, or use a contrasting color if color 1 blends too well with your fabric. This outline is your positioning guide and you need to be able to clearly see it.

4. When the machine stops, remove the Steam-A-Seam paper from the back of the applique and align the fabric within the guide stitches as accurately as possible.

5. Select an appropriate Sulky thread color and restart machine to tack the applique into position (see Tip 1).

6. Continue the embroidery until the design is complete.

7. Trim the backing close to the stitching.

8. To activate the fusible product, press according to package directions. Caution: be sure to consider the fabrics you are pressing to make sure the heat will not cause any damage.

9. Repeat the process to add the second applique.

> **Tip 1:**
> Slow the machine down at this point. If the applique should shift during the sewing, it's easier to catch it and stop it if the machine is not sewing full tilt. Resume your speed once the tack down is complete.

> **Tip 2:**
> Always trim any jump threads at the color changes. This way, the thread tails won't become embedded in later stitches.

5   Apply Appliques to Middle Pocket

1. Using the part of the large bath towel that we cut off in step 2, applique 3 more sea critters following steps on previous page. Center each within its own third of the pocket width and about halfway vertically. The woven edge (instead of the terry edge) is the bottom, which makes it easier to turn since there is less bulk - even more important if you choose to use the pleated pockets.

2. When all embroidery is complete, remove the embroidery unit, and replace embroidery foot with regular sewing foot.

6   Make Applique Templates for Free-Motion Embroidery

Here's another place where you can add your own touch. The sample uses a pieced strip created from 2.5 x 3.5 blocks of coordinating fabrics. You may choose to use one fabric that looks more watery.

1. Trace the wave pattern (from pattern sheet #4) onto the Quilter's Template Plastic and cut it out.

2. Use the plastic template to trace the pattern onto Pattern Ease™. (Your wave can go in either direction.)

3. With right sides together, use regular sewing thread to stitch the Pattern Ease to the wave strip; use a short stitch to facilitate turning.

4. Grade and notch the seam allowance, turn right side out, finger press, then press with an iron.

Apply Applique Wave to Terry Cloth 7

As illustrated in figure 1, the selvage is the bottom. This edge is thinner and easier to work with when attaching it to the caddy foundation.

1. Align the straight, unfinished edge of the wave along the selvage edge of the towel and pin in place.

2. Using the thread of your choice (Lindee used Sulky Polyester Invisible), attach the wave to the towel with a free-motion applique stitch; slow down your machine speed to improve your accuracy, and pivot around the wave points and curves.

Make Casings and Insert Elastic 8

Tip 3:

Use a straight pin to anchor the tail end of the elastic to keep it from pulling all the way through.

1. Time to make some slight customizing decisions. The towel pockets can be flat (easiest), or you can add some fullness by either easing the pockets into position or by adding pleats or gussets. In either case, determine the width of each pocket from edge to edge of the towel for the terry cloth pockets and the fish net pocket.

2. To make it easier to work with, edge finish the towel pockets by choosing an overedge stitch to compress the terry and reduce raveling; a simple zig-zag works perfectly.

3. Make a casing as you attach the seam binding to the top edge of each towel pocket. Use the bias binding foot, or attach it using your favorite method. Stitch close to the edge of the binding because you will need to thread a piece of elastic though this casing.

4. Cut a piece of elastic for each towel pocket that is 1" shorter than the width of each pocket. Using a safety pin attached to one end of the elastic, thread it through the casing. Stay-stitch the elastic at each end of the casing.

Attach the Fish Net Pocket 9

Broadcloth pocket for hanger (on back).

Top terry cloth pocket with wave appliques is divided into two pockets.

Middle terry cloth pocket with embroidered appliques is divided into three pockets.

Fish net pocket with embroidered appliques is divided into two pockets.

Fig. 2. Layout for pockets and appliques.

1. Align the fish net pocket along the lower edge of the towel caddy. Lay out the pocket either flat or pleated and stitch along the 2 sides and bottom edge of towel using a 1/4" seam allowance and matching sewing thread.

2. Straight stitch up the center of the pocket to separate the one large pocket into two smaller pockets.

3. Trim off any excess fish net in the seam allowance.

139

10   Attach the Top and Middle Terry Cloth Pocket

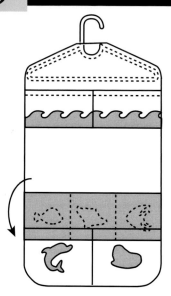

Fig. 3. Attaching the terry cloth pockets.

The middle and top pockets will be attached a little differently than the fish net pocket.

1. Position the middle pocket as desired (fig. 2). Flip the pocket downward horizontally so that the right sides of the pocket and the caddy are together, and the seam line of the bottom edge of the pocket is still aligned in the original position (fig. 3).

2. Stitch the pocket to the caddy by stitching within the selvage edge; this reduces bulk when the pocket is flipped back up.

3. Flip up the pocket and stitch both sides to the edges of the caddy using a zig-zag stitch. With a straight stitch, stitch up to divide the pocket into 3 sections.

4. Attach top terry pocket similarly to the middle pocket. Divide this pocket into two equal sections.

11   Make Hanger Pocket & Seam Binding

Tip:

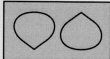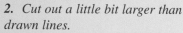

"Windowing" - An Applique Fusing Tip from Marianne Fons & Liz Porter, co-hosts of the PBS TV Show, "Quilting with Fons & Porter"

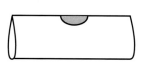

Fig. 4. Make hanger pocket.

Fold the wrong sides of the white cotton fabric together and stitch a small curve about 1/2"- 3/4" in the center for the hanger. Trim out shaded area. Turn, finger press, and press with an iron.

Fig. 5. Attach pocket to back of caddy.

"Windowing" is a nifty way to eliminate the stiffness of fused appliques. Choose a lightweight, "sewable" paper-release fusible. Always read and follow manufacturer's instructions.

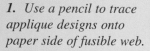

1. Use a pencil to trace applique designs onto paper side of fusible web.

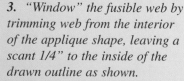

2. Cut out a little bit larger than drawn lines.

3. "Window" the fusible web by trimming web from the interior of the applique shape, leaving a scant 1/4" to the inside of the drawn outline as shown.

4. Follow manufacturer's instructions to fuse web side of each applique shape to wrong side of the applique fabric as shown.

5. Cut out appliques, cutting carefully on drawn outline as shown. Only a thin band of fusible web frames the applique shape.

6. Peel off paper backing; position applique in place on background.

Lay the hanger pocket rectangle over the back of the caddy, matching the top and side edges. Using sewing thread to match or contrast with seam binding, stitch a 1/4" seam along the dotted lines. Trim away excess cotton fabric.

Finish with seam binding.

1. To prepare the raw edges of the terry cloth at the top and corner raw edges, overcast or zig-zag the edges.

2. Bind the outer edge of the caddy the same as you did the pocket edges, taking care **not** to catch the curved cut-out in the hanger pocket.

3. To remove the Solvy from fish net, wash the caddy.

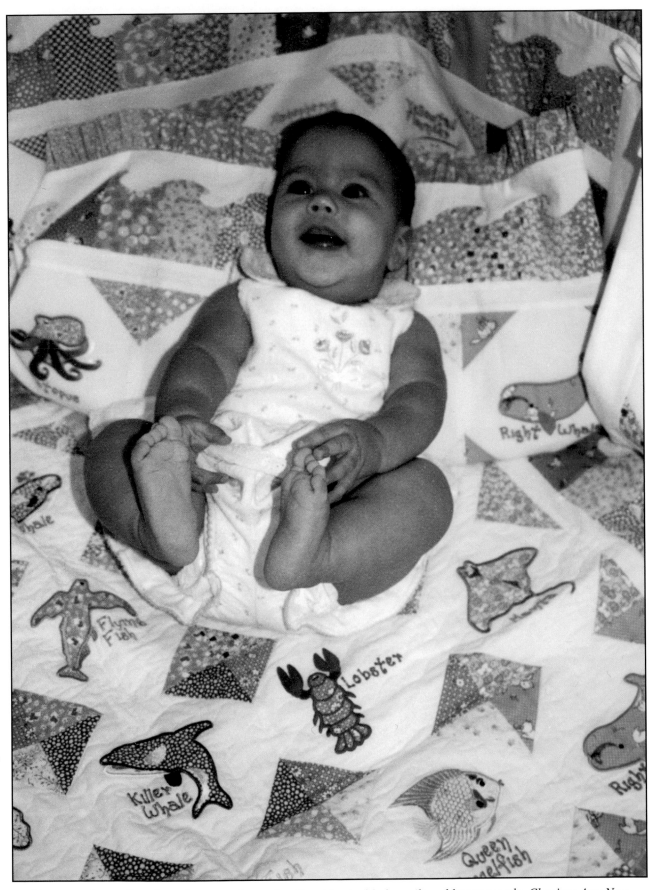

The same Cactus Punch card was used to make this whimsical baby quilt and bumper pads. Charissa Ann Noe,
Joyce and Fred's latest granddaughter, at age 6 months, finds it simply a great place to spend her time.
Make a computer appliqued quilt for your next child, grandchild or friend's babyshower; a perfect gift!

Quick Door Hanger
Applique using
Printer Fabric Sheets

Jamie Fields
*Educational Consultant for
Viking Distributing in
Medford, OR*

*Jamie travels extensively as an
Educational Consultant for
Viking Distributing, teaching
classes and seminars on sewing
and serging.*

*Jamie is a certified
Palmer/Pletsch instructor
for Creative Serging. She is
also a certified Martha Pullen,
Husqvarna Viking Heirloom
Educator and a Quilting From
the Heartland with Husqvarna
Viking quilting instructor.*

*She has been a guest educator
on the "America Sews with Sue
Hausmann" PBS television
show. She enjoys sewing as a
hobby and loves sharing her
ideas and skills with others.*

"I always use Sulky Cut-Away Plus to stabilize this type of project because
it adds a lot of body and stability to the finished item. I also love to trace
my patterns onto Sulky Totally Stable Iron-On Stabilizer and iron the pattern
right onto the fabric. It's nice to be able to use the same pattern over and
over again. I also iron Totally Stable onto slippery fabrics to keep the fabric
from sliding away from the scissors as I'm cutting. While I didn't use
Heat-Away Disintegrating Stabilizer for this project, it is my very favorite
stabilizer to use in my personal clothing for embroidery." --- Jamie

*Above are finished Door Hangers giving their warnings and
welcomes. Left are Sue Hausmann and Jamie on the set of
"America Sews with Sue Hausmann" seen weekly on PBS TV.*

142

1   Preparing the Fabric

1. With a fine-line, permanent-ink marker, trace pattern from pattern sheet #1 onto the non-shiny side of a 9" x 11" piece of Sulky Totally Stable.

2. Iron this pattern (shiny side down) centered on the wrong side of an 11" x 12" piece of fashion fabric.

What You Will Need:

✂ Computer Sewing Machine with Embroidery capabilities and Accessories
✂ 1/3 yd. fashion fabric (cut 4 pieces 11" x 12") for body of door hanger
✂ 2 - 11" squares of white or off-white fabric for inserts
✂ 1 - 9" x 11" piece of Sulky Totally Stable Iron-On Stabilizer
✂ 4 - 12" x 12" pieces of Sulky Cut-Away Plus Stabilizer
✂ 1/4" Ribbon or Cording 14" long
✂ Cotton or Polyester Sewing Thread
✂ Fine-Line, Permanent-Ink Marker
✂ Sulky Threads (for embroidery, applique or other creative stitching)
✂ Fusible web

Using a color copier, the picture was copied onto Husqvarna Viking Colorfast Printer Fabric Sheets.

Pattern for the door hanger is on Pattern Sheet #1.

2   Stitch the Fabric

1. Place 2 pieces of fashion fabric (one with the pattern on top), right sides together, on top of one piece of Sulky Cut-Away Plus Stabilizer.
2. With regular sewing thread and a regular stitch length, straight stitch on inside pattern line.
3. Carefully tear away center of Totally Stable pattern.

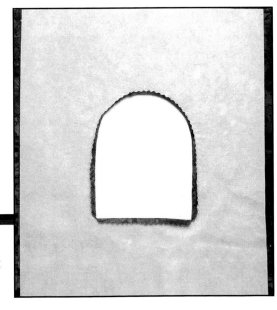

3   Trim

1. Cut away all four layers inside the stitching, 1/4" away from the stitching. (Jamie used pinking shears.) This will leave an opening in the center. Clip curves and corners.
2. Carefully remove the Totally Stable pattern and use it to make a second identical unit. When you carefully remove the Totally Stable Pattern from the second unit, save it for later use.
3. Turn each of the units right side out through their openings and press.

143

4 Embellish Insert

Using the Sulky Decorative Thread of your choice, embellish both of the 11" square insert fabric pieces with the technique of your choice (embroidery, monogramming, applique, free-motion embroidery, decorative stitching); use Cut-Away Plus under the embellishment area to stabilize it. (Jamie used Husqvarna Viking System 5 Customizing Software to create lettering and combine designs.) Center one of the embellished insert fabrics in the opening under one of the fashion fabric units and trim embellished unit, leaving a 1/4" seam allowance. (Serge edges or use a zig-zag stitch to keep from raveling.) Pin and topstitch in place.

wrong side up

right side up

Embroidered over fleece

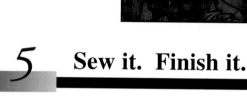

5 Sew it. Finish it.

1. Pin the 1/4" ribbon to the right side of one unit. Place units right sides together, lining up the openings in the center, and pin.

2. Press the saved Totally Stable pattern onto the wrong side of the top unit, lining up center openings. Stitch units together on the outside stitching line. Leaving 1/4" of fabric, trim remaining fabric away around stitching line. Clip curves and corners.

3. Remove the Totally Stable pattern and turn door hanger right side out through the center opening. Press.

4. Center the second embellished unit under the Totally Stable Pattern; press it in place. Cut the fabric around the outside edge of the Totally Stable pattern. Remove the Totally Stable. Serge or finish to a 7-1/2" square. Insert in the other window of the door hanger.

5. Hang on a doorknob or in the center of a door with a small hook. This project can also be used as a picture frame.

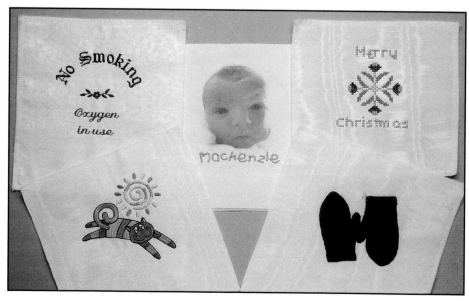

Quick Quilted Photo Frame Pin Cushion
Featuring a Unique Folded 3-D Applique

"As a machine artist I find that I get the best results possible with Sulky threads and stabilizers. They always perform beautifully, regardless of the machine I'm using. I especially like the Sliver threads and the way they perform for me. I wouldn't use anything else." ... Patsy

Patsy Shields
National Director of Education for Sulky of America

Patsy has traveled extensively throughout the U.S. for over 17 years as a free-lance sewing specialist teaching serger classes, fitting workshops, and machine art seminars.

She has been published in the **Serger Update Newsletter** and has contributed to a book for the **Singer Reference Library,** to **Sew News** and the **Patchwork Concepts in Sulky Book** *and the* **Sulky Secrets to Successful Quilting Book,** *as well as co-authoring the* **Updated Serger Concepts in Sulky Book.**

She has taught at National Sewing events including *S.M.A.R.T., Baby Lock Tech, New Home Institute, Singer Academy, Quilt Market and Quilt Festival,* as well as *Sulky Instructor Training Seminars,* and well over a hundred *Sulky "Sew Exciting" Seminars.*

As National Director of Education for Sulky of America, she coordinates Sulky's Educational Activity at trade shows and consumer shows as well as training Sulky Free-Lance Educators to conduct *"Sew Exciting Seminars".*

What You Will Need:

- Sewing Machine
- Sulky KK 2000
  Temporary Spray Adhesive
- Sulky Decorative Threads - your choice
- 1/4 yard each of two fabrics or 2 fat eighths, one light and one dark
- 1 sheet of 2" finished-size Triangle Paper
- Neutral Sewing Thread

- 3" x 4" Piece of Clear Vinyl
- Polyester Stuffing
- 3-4 Tablespoons of Rice
- 1/2" Bias Tape Maker
- Fine-Line, Permanent-Ink Marker
- Ruler, Rotary Cutter, Cutting Mat
- General Sewing Supplies

1 Make the Triangles

1. Cut six triangle squares (2 rows) from the sheet of Triangle Paper (2" finished size).
2. Spray the right side of one of the fabrics with Sulky KK 2000 Temporary Spray Adhesive. Place the 2 fabrics right sides together. Spray the wrong side of the triangle paper with Sulky KK 2000. Place this on the wrong side of the lighter fabric. Cut away the excess fabrics from around the triangle paper.
3. With regular sewing thread, begin straight stitching on one of the dotted lines, and continue until all of the dotted lines are stitched. Use the rotary cutter and ruler to cut thetriangles apart on all the solid lines.
4. Press the seam toward the darker fabric, then remove the Triangle Paper.

2 Combine for Front & Back

1. Divide the blocks into 2 groups of 6 each for the front and back. Arrange the blocks in a pleasing manner. Lots of different combinations/patterns can be formed. You can even create one design for the back and a different one for the front.
2. Using a 1/4" seam, sew the blocks together to make 2 rectangles of 2 blocks x 3 blocks - one for the front and one for the back.

3 Embellish with Sulky Thread

Select a decorative stitch. Use a Sulky Rayon Thread of your choice and embellish over the seam lines and/or design lines of the blocks.

4 Make a Frame

1. From one of the left-over fabrics, make a piece of double-fold bias, approximately 18" to 20" long, to cover the outside edges of the 3" x 4" vinyl "frame". (To make the perfect tape, cut 1" fabric strips on the bias and feed them through a 1/2" bias tape maker.)
2. Cover the two long edges of the vinyl with the bias tape and straight stitch along the top and bottom edges with your Sulky Rayon Thread. Fold the ends of the tape under for a smooth finish.
3. Place the "frame" about 1-1/4" down from the top edge of the right side of the front fabric, and centered between the two sides. Edge-stitch top, bottom and left side only, using the Sulky Rayon Thread.

5 Make a Folded 3-D Applique Flower

1. Cut a 3-1/2" circle from each of the two project fabrics, or use contrasting fabrics. Trim off 1/4" from one of the circles so it is slightly smaller than the other.
2. Divide each circle into fourths by folding each circle in half twice and pressing.

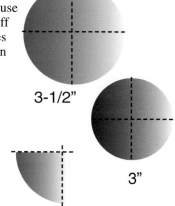

3-1/2"

3"

3. On one circle, fold one creased edge to the center, and continue folding the edges (three times) to the center to form a hexagon (6 sides). Repeat for the other circle.   Press to form sharp edges. Place the smaller hexagon on top of the larger one.

4. Using the Sulky Rayon Thread, tack them together in the center with several small zig-zag stitches at 0 length.

5. Attach the flowers to the top left edge of the frame while making a fuzzy center for the flower by: lowering the feed dogs or putting the stitch length on 0; selecting a wide zig-zag of 6.0 or 7.0; zig-zagging in place several times, stopping in the center of the flower; rotating the fabric slightly and repeating stitching until you have made a "star" pattern; secure stitching by returning to straight stitch and stitching several times in the center. Place scissors under the star zig-zags, close to the outside edge, and snip the threads. Rub the threads with your finger to create a fuzzy look.

6 Complete the Pin Cushion

1. Place the two sets of pieced squares right sides together.

2. Using the neutral sewing thread, begin stitching along one bottom, continuing around sides until you reach the bottom again, leaving an opening to turn. Create a box bottom before turning by stitching across the bottom corners about 1/2" from the edge.

3. Turn, fill with polyester stuffing, then add about 3-4 tablespoons of rice. Poke the rice into the batting so it will be easier to sew the bottom closed.

4. Hand stitch the bottom. When sitting upright, the rice will fall to the bottom and add the needed weight.

5. Insert the picture of your favorite person or pet in the vinyl frame and enjoy!

Slide the photo into the vinyl frame.

7 Other Possibilities

- Use two pieces of fabric 4-1/2" x 7" or one piece 4-1/2" x 14".

- Add appliques to the back either by hand or machine.

- Do random decorative stitching with Sulky Thread all over the fabric, or just rows of decorative stitches.

- Make yo-yos instead of the folded flower and attach them with a decorative button or a covered button.

- Make a ruched flower with a button center.

The possibilities are endless!
Enjoy!

Quick Ornaments and Accessories
Using Sulky Puffy Foam & more!

**Designed by Carol Ingram
and presented on the PBS TV Show
"America Sews with
Sue Hausmann"**

What You Will Need:

- Computerized Embroidery Machine
- Embroidery Cards - Cactus Punch
  Signature Series #61 "Steppin' Out"
  Signature Series #24 "Snow Family"
- Criswald Lace Embroidery Card
- Assorted Sulky 40 wt. Rayon Thread
- Sulky Sliver #8040 Opalescent
- Sulky Invisible Polyester Thread - Clear
- KK 2000 Temporary Spray Adhesive
- Sulky Soft 'n Sheer Stabilizer - White
- Sulky Ultra Solvy Stabilizer
- Sulky 2 mm Puffy Foam in colors
  to match your designs
- Stencil-cutting or wood-burning tool
- Steam Iron & Ironing Surface
- Clear Vinyl - 2 mil
- Rat-tail, Tassels & Pony Beads
- Fabri-Tac™ Glue
- Fusible Web
- Hand Tapestry Needle & Sulky 12 wt. Cotton
- Colored glass ornament
- Ready-made items to put appliques onto
- General Sewing Supplies

The pictures on page 148 show numerous ways that Carol used her designs for:

- Lamps
- Fan pulls
- On Baskets
- Christmas Tree Ornaments
- Stick-ons for glass doors, windows and mirrors,
- On Frames
- Shoes
- Napkin Rings and more!

1. Hoop one layer of Sulky Soft 'n Sheer in your computerized machine embroidery hoop.
2. Cut a piece of White Sulky 2mm Puffy Foam larger than the design area; spray one side with KK 2000 and place in the center of the hoop.
3. Embroider design.

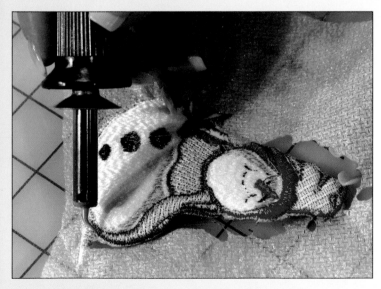

4. Remove from hoop and pull the Puffy Foam away from the design. Cut away the excess Soft 'n Sheer to about 1/8" from the design. If there is any Puffy Foam poking through the design, shrink these little "pokies" away by holding a steam iron about 1" above the design and steaming. This will cause the "pokies" to shrink back into the design.
5. From the wrong side of the design, carefully melt away the remaining Soft 'n Sheer with a wood-burning or stencil-cutting tool. You now have a Free-Form 3-Dimensional Embroidery Design that can be used as an applique in many different decorative ways.

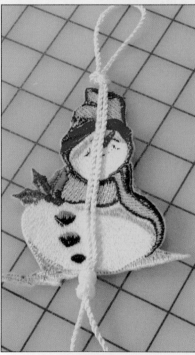

6. To make a hanging cord, cut a 20" piece of purchased rattail cord and fold it in half to make a loop. Tie an overhand knot 3" down from the loop. Lay the cord down the center of the wrong side of one design with the knot at the top. Glue it in place. To pad the snowman's belly, lay a small wad of batting in the center of the design. Slide one or two 4mm plastic beads on the bottom end of cords. Glue them in place at the bottom of the snowman. Glue the wrong side of the stitched out mirrored image design to the wrong side of the first image, sandwiching the cord and batting inside. (Glue the rattail cord around the edge of the design if doing the Shoe on the back cover.)
7. Using Sulky Polyester Invisible Thread, you can stitch it anywhere on a garment, even in places that are hard or impossible to properly hoop. *This is also mistakeless embroidery without the stress of working on a garment.*
8. Hand-stitch onto a pocket that you wouldn't want stitched closed. Glue on home decor items such as lamps, candle holders, and wood items, or plastics such as shoes and purses to make a coordinated outfit!

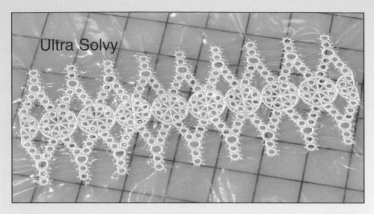

Ultra Solvy

Sulky Ultra Solvy rinses away leaving only the applique or lace!

9. To make a lapel pin, embroider design over Puffy Foam, then glue it to a second piece of matching Puffy Foam; trim, leaving 1/4" of the Puffy Foam showing all around the design. Glue a craft safety pin to the back and wear with pride.

Make the Lace Ornaments

1. Choose the single lace design on the Criswald Embroidery Card which makes one panel of lace. To go all the way around a standard ball ornament, you will need to stitch out three of these designs either joined together using the computer softwear so they stitch out as one panel, or, if you do not have the softwear, stitched together by hand or machine.
2. Hoop Ultra Solvy in the machine embroidery hoop and stitch the design onto the Ultra Solvy with Sulky 30 wt. Cotton #1001 White on top and in the bobbin.
3. Remove from hoop and trim away the larger pieces of Ultra Solvy; immerse in water to dissolve the remaining Ultra Solvy. Lay flat to dry.
4. Using Sulky 12 wt. Cotton #1001 White, hand stitch the three adjacent end points together to form a ball-shaped top. Insert glass ball and close up the bottom as you did the top, encasing the ball inside the lace.

Glass Stick-ons

To make a removable stick-on for windows or any glass surface, cut a piece of table-cloth plastic vinyl (2 mil) to the size and shape of the embroidered design and glue it to the back of the free-form embroidered applique. If it resists sticking, rub the vinyl against your clothes to create a static-cling, and place on the glass surface.

Show ID or Photo Neck Badges
Appliqued with Computer Embroidery

Designed by Joyce Drexler and Evelyn Howard

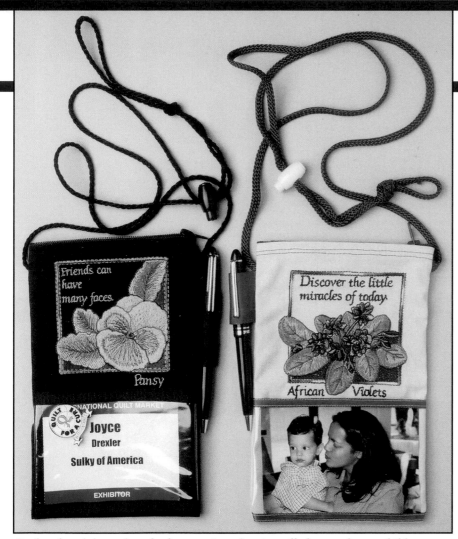

What You Will Need:

- Sewing Machine with edge foot
- "Inspirational Concepts in Sulky" AD3000 Embroidery Card designed by Joyce Drexler for Amazing Designs®
- Sulky 40 wt. Rayon Threads as suggested in chosen design
- 1-2/3 yd. of cording with cord stop
- 3-1/2" x 7" piece of 2 mil vinyl for window
- 2 - 1/4" x 7" pieces of ribbon to match or contrast with fabric
- 1-1/2" wide x 2-1/2" to 2-3/4" long grosgrain ribbon (same color as 1/4" ribbon) for pen holder
- 1/4 yd. of Sulky Tear-Easy Stabilizer
- 9" zipper to coordinate with fabric
- 1 - 9" x 12" heavy cotton fabric for front (to be trimmed after embroidery)
- 1 - 6" x 9" heavy cotton for back of badge
- General Sewing Supplies

Perfect for club or show badges, or just showing off photos of your children or pets when you use it as a "hands-free" purse for shopping.

Preparation

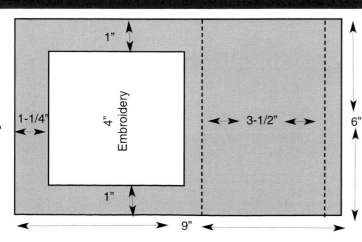

1. Choose your favorite 4" embroidery design. Joyce used designs from her Amazing Designs® Inspirational Card AD3000. On the 9" x 12" heavy cotton fabric, position and stitch a 4" embroidery as shown in the illustration. Trim to 6" x 9" allowing 1-1/4" at the top and 1" on each side of the embroidery.

2. Serge or overcast stitch the raw edges of both 6" x 9" pieces that will be the front and back of the badge holder.

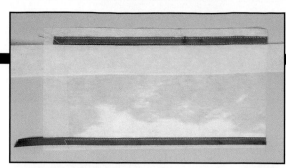

1

1. Lay a 3-1/2" x 7" piece of 2 mil window vinyl lengthwise on top of a 4-1/2" x 8" piece of Tear-Easy. With the edges matching, place a 7" piece of 1/4" ribbon on top of one 7" side of the vinyl. To help your presser foot move smoothly over the vinyl, with the ribbon and the plastic edges to the left, place a 1" x 8" strip of Tear-Easy over the vinyl, butted up to the right edge of the ribbon, **not** over it; do not stitch on this strip. Use an edge foot to stitch both long edges of the ribbon to the vinyl. Repeat for the other side of the vinyl, but only stitch the inside edge (the other edge will be stitched when it is attached to the front).

2. Remove all Tear-Easy, trim ribbon-covered window to 6" and place it 1/2" from the bottom of the embroidered "front". Use a regular sewing foot to baste both sides within the overcast edges.

3. Place the closed 9" zipper, upside down lengthwise, across a 6" edge of the "back" fabric, with the bottom end of the zipper aligned with the right hand corner. Use a zipper foot to stitch them together 1/8" from the outside edge; the remaining 3" of the zipper hangs off the left side.

2

1. With right sides together, stitch the top of the embroidered "front" to the other side of the zipper, 1/8" from the edge.

2. Fold the wide grosgrain ribbon (for the pen holder) in half and place it on the right edge of the front, keeping the top of the ribbon even with the top of the embroidery; baste in place.

3. Use an edge foot to stitch the second line of stitching on the bottom of the ribbon, 1/8" from the edge, creating a window pocket.

3

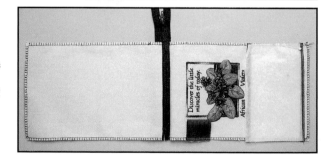

1. Using the zipper foot edge as a guide and the center needle position, topstitch both sides of the zipper with a matching Sulky 40 wt. Rayon, then add another row of stitching below them using the left needle position.

2. Place the cording just below the zipper on the right side of the "front" and pin in place allowing 2" to extend to the outside from each side (the bulk of the cording is heaped in the center of the front).

   Tip: Put tape along both bottom edges of the cording to keep them from raveling.

4

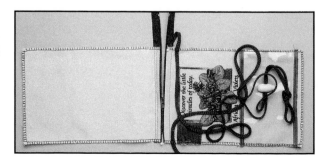

1. **Open the zipper to the middle of the bag and put the right sides together.** With the "front" on top, start at the right top corner and stitch a 3/8" seam around the three sides of the badge holder, ending at the other side of the zipper. Be sure to start and stop by backstitching several times within 1/8" of the zipper coils. Clip corners.

2. Fold the 2" cord down along the 3/8" seam allowance and use a narrow zig-zag to stitch down the remaining length of the cording.

3. With the zipper open, clip off the excess of the zipper leaving about 1" extending. Fold this remaining extension down 90 degrees and straight stitch it into the seam allowance. Turn right side out.

Quick Lattice Pockets using Ultra Solvy as a foundation

Designed by Carol Ingram and *presented on the PBS TV Show – Martha's Sewing Room with Martha Pullen*

"The new Sulky Ultra Solvy is so incredibly durable that techniques like this lattice pocket, which involve a great deal of heavy stitching and even additional applique, can be done on one layer. No perforations." Carol

What You Will Need:

- ✂ Sewing Machine with Computer Embroidery capabilities
- ✂ Cording or Piping Foot
- ✂ Sulky Ultra Solvy™
- ✂ Sulky KK 2000™ Temporary Spray Adhesive
- ✂ Tulle or Netting cut larger than the desired size of pocket
- ✂ Fine-line, permanent-ink black marker
- ✂ Ruler with a 45 degree angle
- ✂ Gimp Cord
- ✂ Sulky Threads (for embroidery, applique or other creative stitching)
- ✂ Sulky 40 wt. Rayon Thread #1005 Black
- ✂ Sulky Soft 'n Sheer™ Stabilizer
- ✂ Computer Embroidery Card - Carol used her Cactus Punch Signature Series #61 "Steppin' Out"
- ✂ Sulky 2mm Puffy Foam™ - color to closely match design threads
- ✂ Wood Burning Tool or Stencil Cutter
- ✂ Sulky Polyester Invisible Thread
- ✂ General Sewing Supplies

"Color Blocking" with computer embroidered shoe pockets over a stitched lattice gives a summer airy look to this sand-washed rayon jacket. The jacket (pattern by Martha Pullen Co.) was created by Carol Ingram using her Steppin' Out embroidery card by Cactus Punch™.

153

1   Create the Ultra Solvy Grid

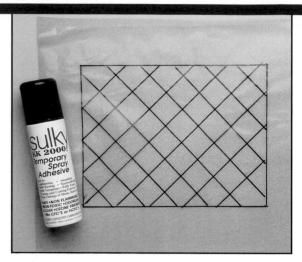

1. Cut a piece of Ultra Solvy 3" larger overall than the pocket size desired. (Carol made <u>two</u> 6" x 8" pockets.) Cut the same size piece of tulle or netting.

2. Using a fine-line, permanent-ink, black marker and a ruler, draw the pocket size and shape of your choice onto the Ultra Solvy.

3. Use a ruler with a 45 degree angle and the fine-line, permanent-ink marker to draw diagonal lines approximately 1" apart across the drawn pattern in both directions.

2   Apply the Gimp Cord

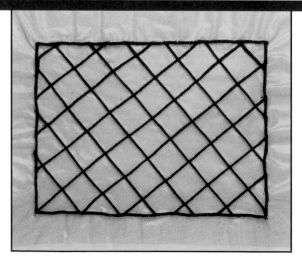

1. Using Sulky KK 2000 Temporary Spray Adhesive, lightly spray the Ultra Solvy and lay the tulle or netting over it.

2. Thread the top and bobbin with Sulky 40 wt. Rayon Thread #1005 Black, and attach a cording or piping foot to the machine.

3. Lay the gimp cord or other heavyweight cord over one of the drawn lines and sew a 3mm wide satin stitch over it. Leave approximately 1/2" of gimp extending beyond the end of each row, to be clipped off later. Satin stitch over cord on all lines, in both directions.

3   Complete the Lattice

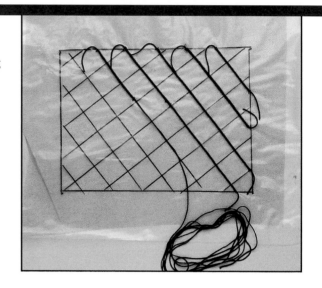

1. Clip off all extended tails. Lay the cord around the outside of the sewn grid and satin stitch over it, catching and covering the clipped ends of each row as you stitch. Stitch completely around the grid. Increase your satin stitch to 4mm and go around the outside of the grid once again to secure the ends.

2. Apply any computerized machine embroidery design onto the grid and proceed to Step 6 (or see steps 4 and 5 to learn how to make a "Free-Form", Computer-Embroidered Applique).

4 — Make a "Free-Form" Applique

To make a more 3-dimensional, "Free-Form" design to applique onto the lattice pocket:

1. Hoop one layer of Sulky Soft 'n Sheer Stabilizer.

2. Spray KK 2000 onto a piece of Sulky Puffy Foam matched in color and size to the chosen design, and place it on the hooped stabilizer where the design will stitch out.

3. Using Sulky Threads, embroider entire shoe design (or other design of your choice). *Carol used her Cactus Punch Signature Series Card #61, "Steppin Out".*

5 — Appliqueing the Design

1. Pull away excess Puffy Foam. Cut away the Soft 'n Sheer close to the design. Use a wood burning tool or stencil cutter to carefully melt away excess Soft 'n Sheer around the edges of the design. *If any Puffy Foam peeks out between the stitches of the design, give the entire design a burst of steam from a hot iron held slightly above the Puffy Foam design to shrink the "pokies" into the stitching.*

2. Spray the back of the "free-form" applique design with KK 2000 and place it where desired on the grid.

3. Attach an applique foot, set machine for a 2mm width and length zig-zag, and use Sulky Clear Invisible Polyester Thread to stitch the applique in place.

6 — Attaching the Pocket

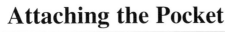

1. Cut or tear away tulle or netting from around the outside edges of the grid.

2. Trim away excess Ultra Solvy from around the grid pocket and place it in tepid water, covering it completely. Soak 5 to 10 minutes to completely dissolve the Ultra Solvy. Rinse thoroughly. Blot dry with a towel and lay aside to dry completely.

3. Iron Totally Stable onto the reverse side of the garment where the pocket will be placed; if the fabric is thin or flimsy, use two layers of Totally Stable.

4. When the "Grid Pocket" is dry, spray KK 2000 on the wrong side of the grid and temporarily adhere it onto the garment. Use Black Sulky 40 wt. Rayon or Sulky Smoke Invisible Thread and a short, narrow zig-zag stitch to stitch around the outside of the pocket, leaving open at the top.

Phone Book or Photo Binder Cover
Applique the House

Designed by Beverly Johnson

This phone book or photo album cover offers a 9" x 11" area for embellishment and makes a great house-warming or shower gift as well as a practical cover for your own phone book.

Project directions are for a phone book or photo album cover 9" wide x 11" high and 2-3/8" thick, but the finished size can easily fit your specific needs by altering the depth of the spine.

The cover can be lined with either plain fabric or the cover fabric. Beverly likes to put batting or fusible fleece under the main fabric to add body and keep the color of the phone book from showing through.

What You Will Need:

- ✂ Zig-Zag Sewing Machine
- ✂ Open-Toe Applique Foot
- ✂ Cut one rectangle of main fabric: 13" high by 34" wide
- ✂ Cut one piece of lining, which could be the same fabric: 13" by 20"
- ✂ Cut one piece of batting or fusible fleece 13" x 20-3/8"
- ✂ Small pieces of an assortment of fabrics for applique

- ✂ Paper-Backed Fusible Web
- ✂ Sulky Tear-Easy, Totally Stable or Stiffy Stabilizer
- ✂ Sulky Decorative Threads of your choice
- ✂ Chalk Marker
- ✂ Fine-line, Permanent-Ink Marker
- ✂ Patterns on pattern sheet #3
- ✂ General Sewing Supplies

Preparing the Fabric 1

1. Following the pattern on Pattern Sheet #3, mark the lines on your 13" x 34" main fabric with a chalk marker as indicated. Seam allowances are included in these measurements. The dotted lines at the top and bottom are 1" from the cut edges and should be 11" apart.

The section marked "D" is the area for embellishment (the front of the book cover). The actual size of the finished front cover is 9" x 11".

Preparing Appliques 2

1. Use a fine-line, permanent-ink marker to trace the house and shrub shapes from pattern sheet #3 onto the paper side of the fusible web. (The pattern is already reversed.)

2. Fuse the web to the back of the desired fabrics. Cut out the shapes and fuse them in position onto Section "D". Make sure things are level.

3. Place either Sulky Tear-Easy, Totally Stable or Stiffy Stabilizer behind the fabric in section "D". Only do the applique work in this area, remembering that the actual size of the finished cover is 9" x 11"; the rest of the fabric is seam allowance. Avoid these edges or your decorative stitching will disappear into the seams.

Set up the Machine for Satin Stitching 3

1. Thread the top and bobbin with a Sulky 40 wt. Rayon to match the color of the fabric. Select a medium width zig-zag at whatever length setting produces a pleasing satin stitch on your machine.

TIP: You could also use Sulky Black or White Polyester Bobbin Thread or Sulky Polyester Invisible Thread in the bobbin to avoid thread color changes.

2. Go around each raw edge, starting with the background elements and working forward to the foreground. The trees are background, the house is midground, and the steps and shrub to the left are foreground.

3. To make the trees more natural looking, use a Sulky 40 wt. Variegated Rayon Thread and a decorative type satin stitch like the "grass" stitch or "ragged edge" satin stitch, but others can be used with great results. *Play with your stitches.*

4. Use a decorative stitch such as a leaf or vine-type design to stitch vines with Sulky UltraTwist Rayon #3041 going up the side of the house. To make bartack flowers on the vines and in the shrubbery, use Sulky 30 wt. Variegated Yellow #2117.

5. Use a zig-zag at the widest width and set the length to zero (or lower the feed dogs).

6. Stitch about 5 to 8 stitches in place, then stop with the needle in the fabric on the left side.

7. Raise the presser foot, pivot the fabric about 1/5 of a turn and lower the foot. Stitch another 5 to 8 stitches, again leaving the needle in the fabric on the left. Each time the foot is raised, pivot 1/5 of a turn. Repeat 5 times.

8. Varying the width of the stitch will produce larger or smaller flowers. *Easy, fun flowers.*

Construct the Book Cover 4

1. Once the embellishment is done, remove the stabilizer and press well. Hem the two short ends and stitch them down, making about a 1/4" turn under. Fuse the fleece to the wrong side of the cover, positioning it from the left of section "B" to the right of section "D". The batting covers the front, back and the spine of the book.

2. Lay the book cover right side up on a flat surface and fold sections "A" and "E" to the fold lines. Lay the lining on top of this with the right side of the lining facing the right side of the book cover. Don't be alarmed by the raw edges of the lining, they will all be hidden shortly.

3. Use a ruler to mark a horizontal straight line 1" down from the top edge, and one more 11" down from that, making sure the lines are square with the folded edges. Straight stitch with matching thread along these two lines. Turn the book cover right side out and press. Stitch along the marked spine lines.

4. Insert your phone book and use it to call someone and tell them what a great job you did.

Happy Cats Quilt
Satin Stitched Cats

Designed and Quilted by Beverly Johnson

Beverly Johnson
Sulky Canadian
National Educator

Beverly began her career teaching Garment Design and Construction, and then moved on to a Home Interiors business. A long distance move also brought about a career change; she started Bra-makers Supply, the premier source for bra-making supplies for the home sewist. Beverly teaches bra-making, has authored two books and is a frequent contributor to "Threads" Magazine.
She co-authored the book *Trans-Canada Stitches Guide*, and has written several technical instruction manuals for the drapery making business. She is currently working on a bra-making instruction book.

Embellishment has always been a big part of the reason she loves to sew and Sulky threads have been her doorway to greater creativity. She became the Canadian National Educator for Sulky in 1999 and she travels all over Canada conducting Sew Exciting Seminars.

Beverly lives in Brampton, Ontario in a sewing room surrounded by a house which she shares with two cats. The cats, while interested in the threads, are not much help in the design process.

"When I first started using Sulky threads back in 1987, I only had 50 beautiful colors to choose from and I thought I was in Thread Heaven! Now, with 337 colors, I can't believe how easy it is to match fabric colors with subtle differences like the grayscale cat quilts I've done here.
Matching these 9 tones of gray was easy! Each cat is appliqued in Sulky 40 wt. Rayon Thread and the quilting is done with 30 wt. Rayon. I love having the different weight threads for different areas of the quilt. Using 30 wt. for the quilting makes the stitching stand out, while the finer 40 wt. around the appliques adds a wonderful satin edge. Sulky threads perform beautifully like the Heavenly threads they are!" -- Beverly

1 Preparing the Fabrics

1. Out of either the black or white background fabric, cut: eight 9" squares; three 10" squares, each of which you cut in half diagonally to form 6 half-square triangles; and one 10-1/2" square which you cut in half diagonally, then in half again to form 4 quarter-square triangles.
2. Trace 7 cat shapes (without faces) from Pattern Sheet #1 onto the paper side of the fusible web. Trace one additional cat (holding the yarn ball) onto the fusible web. (The patterns are already reversed.)
3. Rough cut the cat shapes and fuse the cat with the ball onto either the white or black fabric; fuse each of the rest onto the back of a different grayscale fabric.
4. Because we will place all squares on the diagonal in this quilt, cut out the 8 cats and fuse each of them "on point" to the 8 background fabric 9" squares. Make sure the paws are reasonably level and the whole cat is about 1" in from each side of the square.

2 Cat's Faces

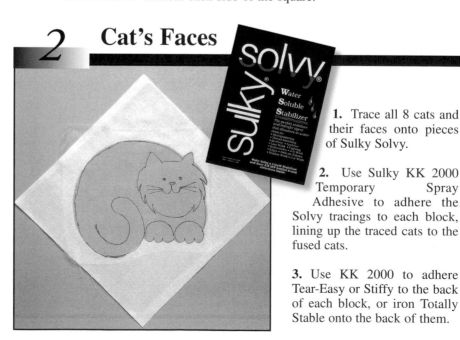

1. Trace all 8 cats and their faces onto pieces of Sulky Solvy.

2. Use Sulky KK 2000 Temporary Spray Adhesive to adhere the Solvy tracings to each block, lining up the traced cats to the fused cats.

3. Use KK 2000 to adhere Tear-Easy or Stiffy to the back of each block, or iron Totally Stable onto the back of them.

3 Satin Stitch Applique

1. **Set up your machine for a satin stitch:**
   - Attach the open-toe applique foot.
   - Select the zig-zag stitch with a 4 width and 1 length (or whatever length setting that gives you a close satin stitch).
   - Thread the bobbin with either white or black Sulky Bobbin Thread to best match the different shades of gray Sulky 40 wt. Rayon Thread on top (begin with the lightest shade).

2. Start at the area under the cat's chin and continue around the paws in a figure 8 pattern. Finish where the paw joins the front of the body. Tie off. *Note: For greater visibility in our samples to the right, we did the first stitching in blue thread and the partially completed second stitching in red thread.*

3. With the same color thread, start at the base of the tail and continue over the back and around the head and ears. Taper the stitch width to zero at each "point" on the face. End where the ear meets the body. Tie off.

4. Narrow the satin stitch to a width of 1 to do the whiskers, and a width of 2 to form the mouth. Stitch the eyes by starting at a width of 0-1 and tapering up to a width of 4-5 and back to 0-1 to form a circle. If your machine has circles built in, that would be a good stitch to use. Beverly used one built-in heart decorative stitch for each cat's nose.

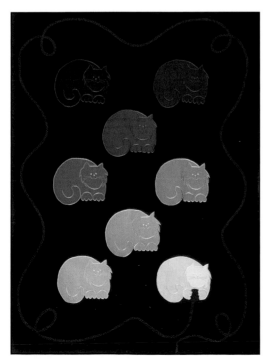

What You Will Need:

- ✄ Sewing Machine
- ✄ Open-Toe Applique Foot and Edge Foot
- ✄ If you are using the white background, the fabrics you will need are:
  - 2-1/2 yds. White fabric for blocks, borders, binding and backing
  - 8 fat quarters of grayscale fabrics running from light gray to black
  - 1/4 yd. of red for the bias yarn and ball
- ✄ If you are using the black background, the fabrics you will need are:
  - 2-1/2 yds. Black fabric for blocks, borders, binding and backing
  - 8 fat quarters running from white to dark gray
  - 1/4 yd. of red for the bias yarn and ball
- ✄ Fusible Web with release sheet
- ✄ Sulky Solvy Water Soluble Stabilizer
- ✄ Sulky Tear-Easy, Sulky Stiffy or Sulky Totally Stable Stabilizer
- ✄ Sulky KK 2000 Temporary Spray Adhesive
- ✄ Sulky Bobbin Thread
- ✄ Sulky 40 wt. Rayon Thread:
  - #1002 Soft White (if using black background)
  - #1234 Almost Black (if using white background)
  - #1147 Xmas Red
  - #1325 Whisper Gray
  - #1327 Dk. Whisper Gray
  - #1328 Nickel Gray
  - #1329 Dk. Nickel Gray
  - #1166 Med. Steel Gray
  - #1220 Charcoal Gray
  - #1240 Smokey Gray
- ✄ 30 wt. Sulky Rayon Thread
  - #1002 Soft White for white background or #1234 Almost Black for black background
- ✄ General Sewing Supplies

5. Change the thread for each cat to make the colors run smoothly from light to dark.

Tip:

If your faces look a little different from each other, don't worry about it...it just gives them personality.

Finished size 31" x 43"

Remove the Stabilizers

1. When the faces are complete, the Solvy can be removed with a Q-TIP *(Quick Tool Imminently Proper for Solvy Removal)* dipped in water and run over the stitches. Remove the stabilizer from the back of the blocks.

1. Join the blocks as pictured on page 28, using the half-square and quarter-square triangles to fill in the areas around the cat blocks. Place the cat holding the ball at the lower right-hand corner. Trim off any uneven excess with a rotary cutter. Add 4" wide borders all around.

 ## Add the Bias Yarn

1. Once the borders are added, make the bias yarn by cutting 1" bias strips from the red fabric with a rotary cutter, and stitching them together to get the length desired; then turn under the long edges in thirds, keeping all raw edges underneath. Press.

2. Starting at the ball, pin the bias yarn all around the outside edges of the border and curling back around to the ball as shown in the quilt. Topstitch the yarn in place with Sulky 40 wt. Rayon Thread #1147 Xmas Red, using an edge-stitch foot to keep the stitching as close to the edge of the yarn as possible. Tie a knot in the bias yarn at the end and cut 1" beyond the knot. Press the quilt top and trim it back to a rectangular shape.

Layer the Quilt

1. Cut a backing 3" larger all around than the finished size of the quilt. Cut a thin, lightweight batting the same size as the finished quilt. Center the quilt top on the batting and backing. Secure the layers with Sulky KK 2000. Stipple quilt with either #1001 White or #1005 Black Sulky 30 wt. Rayon Thread around each cat and around the border, being careful not to stitch through the yarn.

2. Once finished, wrap the backing around to the front of the quilt in a fold-over miter. This binding method is quick and easy and does not need a separate binding to be cut. When the binding is pinned in place, use a blanket stitch and the Sulky 30 wt. Rayon Thread to secure the binding by machine. ALL DONE and not a single hand-stitch anywhere!

Enjoy your happy new litter.

Seasonal Embroideryscapes™
used as Blanket Stitched Appliques

Designed by Joyce Drexler
using Amazing Designs™ Seasonal Inspirations Scape 1 - Embroideryscapes ES-202.

Embroideryscapes Package
ES-202 contains:
Transfer and Embroidery
Design Projects, 4 Heat Transfers,
Templates, 31 Designs on 3-1/2" floppy
disks with complete instructions.

These great looking embroidered scenes can be done on almost any computerized embroidery machine. Iron the full-color transfer to a background fabric of your choice for each season. Stabilize and secure in a hoop. Follow package instructions for lining up embroideries. To finish the scene, any of the four seasonal embroideries can be stitched over the transfer with the recommended Sulky 40 wt. Rayon colors. Once embroidered, trim background fabric to desired size. Turn under edges and blanket stitch onto your favorite jacket, sweatshirt or jumper. They can also be used as quilt blocks, pillows, wallhangings or framed. Because of the amount of stitching, stabilize the background fabric with several layers of Sulky Tear-Easy. A large machine embroidery needle is used (at least a 14/90 or 16/100) since you must go through the transfer ink. These Embroidery scapes are not recommended for lightweight fabrics. Look for them at your local sewing machine or fabric store, or see Sources on page 164.

Endless Possibilities!

Computer Embroidered Covers for Binders/ Photo Albums/ Scrapbooks

by Joyce Drexler
featuring designs from her Inspirational Embroidery Cards AD 3000 & AD 3009
and Seasonal Embroideryscapes ES 202 produced by Amazing Designs™

What You Will Need:

- ✂ Sewing Machine with Embroidery capabilities
- ✂ 90/14 embroidery needle and a 90/14 metallic needle
- ✂ Sulky Holoshimmer or Sliver Thread and Sulky Polyester Invisible Thread
- ✂ Chalk Marker
- ✂ Rotary Cutter, Mat and Ruler
- ✂ Iron and Pressing Surface

- ✂ Fabrics:
  - • Cut the book cover fabric 4" higher and 3-4 times wider than the front of the book you wish to cover
  - • Cut Sulky Cut-Away Plus Stabilizer the same size as the fabric
  - • Fleece and Backing Fabric cut the same size as above
- ✂ Regular sewing thread to match book cover fabric
- ✂ Sulky KK 2000 Temporary Spray Adhesive
- ✂ Sulky 40 wt. Rayon Threads to coordinate with book fabric and as suggested by the embroidery card
- ✂ General Sewing Supplies

1 Prepare Book Cover Fabric

Cut your chosen book cover fabric 4" higher and 3 to 4 times wider than the front of the book you wish to cover. With wrong sides together, fold in half widthwise and finger press the fold line. Place fold line to the left. Open the book to its center page and lay it on the fabric so the center of the book's spine is on the fold line; center the book top to bottom. Close the book to the right and trace around it with a chalk marker. Find the center of the marked outline and draw intersecting vertical and horizontal lines to match with the center of your chosen embroidery design.

2   Stabilize and Embroider the Book Cover

Cut a piece of Sulky Cut-Away Plus the same size as the book cover fabric, spray it with KK 2000, and smooth the wrong side of the fabric on top of it. Hoop, centering the cross in the center of the hoop. Embroider the design with the suggested Sulky 40 wt. Rayon Threads, remove the fabric from the hoop, and press.

3   Channel Quilt

Layer the backing fabric, thin batting, and book cover fabric using KK 2000 to hold them together. If your fabric has lines like bricks or stripes, simply follow the lines in the fabric. If not, draw them with a chalk marker using the top and bottom of the embroidery design border as a guide to draw a line on either side of the border to the edges (indicated by dotted line).

Thread a 90/14 metallic needle with Sulky Sliver or Holoshimmer and put a Sulky 40 wt. Rayon Thread (color to match the fabric) in the bobbin. Straight stitch quilt on the chalk line, then use the edge of the presser foot to stitch parallel lines from the center out. You may want to draw several extra lines parallel to the center one to help you keep the quilting lines straight.

White lines indicate where the front cover is located.

Solid white lines on photo above indicate flaps and spine.

Trim and Overcast   4

Cut off the full width of the top and bottom, 1/2" outside the outline of the book front. Wrap the embroidered fabric around the book with the embroidered design centered on the front cover. Fold the fly covers inside the book. Pin mark the front and back folds. Pin mark where you want the flaps to end, matching the length of the front and back. Remove the book and, with cover right side up, cut off ends square at the 2 outside pins. Using a serger or an overlock stitch and foot on your regular sewing machine, stitch around all 4 sides with a matching Sulky Rayon on top and regular sewing thread in the bobbin.

Turn Right Side Out   5

With the right side up, fold in the flap ends at the pins you placed to mark the edges of the book cover. Pin in place and use Sulky Polyester Invisible Thread to sew along the top and bottom edges of the flap portion 3/8" from the edge; backstitch securely at the beginning and the end.

Turn right side out. From the back side, turn down the top and bottom edges to the inside and use Sulky Invisible Thread to top stitch them in place with 2 lines of straight stitching or 1 line of zig-zag stitching.

Insert the binder or photo album. This makes a very thoughtful gift for a special someone.

Turn up edge.
Pin. Stitch.

NEW! 13" x 13" x 2" deep

Empty or
7 Assortments Available
Holds 104 Sulky Small Spools

Sulky Slimline Storage Box™

NEW!

250YD-225M

250YD-225M

24 brilliant colors! See page 12.

HOLOSHIMMER HOLOSHIMMER

Sulky Holoshimmer™ MetallicThread

NEW!

66 Matte Colors in both heavy 12 wt. and 30 wt. King Spools

Premium **Sulky®**
30 WT. ALL-PURPOSE MERCERIZED COTTON
500 yds/450 m
MATTE FINISH, STRONG, MACHINE OR HAND USE, WASHABLE & DRY CLEANABLE

Sulky 12 wt. & 30 wt. Cotton Thread

SOURCES:

*Look for items used in this book
at your favorite sewing, quilting, fabric or craft store.
If unavailable, contact the following sources:*

MAIL & ON-LINE ORDER SOURCE

• **For the complete line of Sulky Products including:**
All Threads - Cotton, Rayon, Metallic, Invisible, Polyester,
Holoshimmer™ - virtually all in large and small spools.
All Sulky Stabilizers - most in 1 yd. pkgs.,
8" rolls, 12" rolls and 25 yd. bolts.
"Real" Thread Color Charts, Sulky Books, KK 2000,
Puffy Foam and Sulky Iron-on Transfer Pens
New! Slimline Storage Box™ & Sulky Paper Solvy™

• *Plus many other products used in this book:*
  • **Rainbow™ Color Wheel**   • **Quilter's Rulers**
  • **Triangle Paper**   • **Machine Needles**
  • **Teflon Pressing Sheets**
  • **Rotary Cutters & Cutting Mats**
  • **German Hardwood Machine Embroidery Hoops**

• *Joyce Drexler's Designer Embroidery Cards:*
  • **Inspirational Floral Embroidery Card AD-3000**
  • **UltraTwist Seasonal Card AD-3002**
  • **Inspirational Pressed Leaves Embro. Card AD-3009**
  • **Seasonal Embroideryscapes™ Transfer
     & Embroidery Card ES-202**
  • **Cactus Punch® Signature Series #77 - Autumn;**
     Also Winter, Spring and Summer when available

• *Carol Ingram's Cactus Punch Signature Series
     Embroidery Cards:*
  • **Noah's Ark #07**   • **Holiday Trapunto #05**
  • **Snow Family #22**   • **Winter Scenes #23**
  • **Steppin' Out #61**   • **Steppin' Out with Style #65**
                 • **Snow Globes #85**

• *Carol Ingram's Snow Follies Fabric by Fabric Traditions*

SPEED STITCH, INC. - 1-800-874-4115
3113 Broadpoint Dr., Punta Gorda, FL 33983
Fax: 1-941-743-4634
ORDER ONLINE: www.speedstitch.com

QUILTING SERVICES:

*To have your quilts quilted with Sulky Thread on a long-arm
quilting machine by one of the professionals that quilted
samples for this book, contact:*

Evelyn Howard
27182 Townsend Terr.
Harbor Heights, FL 33983
ejquilts@home.com
941-764-0499

Marilyn Badger
Oregon Coast Quilting
15957 Hwy. 101 So. Suite 3
Brookings, OR 97415
541-469-9122

NATIONAL NONWOVENS®
P. O. Box 150
Easthampton, MA 01027
e-mail: sales@nationalnonwovens.com

JO SONJA'S® FABRIC PAINT
Chroma Acrylics, Inc.
205 Bucky Drive, Lititz, PA 17543
717-626-8866 - www.chroma.com

CACTUS PUNCH, INC.®
1101 W. Grant, Suite 202, Tucson, AZ 85705
520-622-8460   www.cactuspunch.com

AMAZING DESIGNS®
Call the toll-free Dealer Locator Number
888-874-6760 or check the website:
www.amazingdesigns.com